*American Women Scientists*

ALSO BY MOIRA DAVISON REYNOLDS

*Immigrant American Women Role Models*
(McFarland, 1997)

*Women Advocates of Reproductive Rights*
(McFarland, 1994)

*Women Champions of Human Rights*
(McFarland, 1991)

*Nine American Women of the Nineteenth Century*
(McFarland, 1988)

Uncle Tom's Cabin *and Mid-Nineteenth Century United States*
(McFarland, 1985)

# American Women Scientists

*23 Inspiring Biographies,
1900–2000*

*by*
Moira Davison Reynolds

McFarland & Company, Inc., Publishers
*Jefferson, North Carolina, and London*

*The present work is a reprint of the illustrated case bound edition of* American Women Scientists: 23 Inspiring Biographies, 1900–2000, *first published in 1999 by McFarland.*

LIBRARY OF CONGRESS CATALOGUING-IN-PUBLICATION DATA

Reynolds, Moira Davison.
    American women scientists: 23 inspiring biographies, 1900–2000 /
by Moira Davison Reynolds.
        p.    cm.
    Includes bibliographical references and index.

    ISBN 0-7864-2161-4 (softcover : 50# alkaline paper)

    1. Women scientists — United States — Biography.   2. Women
scientists — United States — History — 20th century.   I. Title.
Q141.R44   2004
509.2'273 — dc21                                                    99-14603
[B]

British Library cataloguing data are available

On the cover: (top) ©2004 Corbis Images; (left) Experimental
nuclear physicist Chien-Shiung Wu (courtesy AIP Emilio Segre
Visual Archives); Astronomer Annie Jump Cannon (courtesy
Harvard College Observatory)

Manufactured in the United States of America

*McFarland & Company, Inc., Publishers*
   *Box 611, Jefferson, North Carolina 28640*
      *www.mcfarlandpub.com*

To the memory of
Catherine Frances Conway MacPherson,
longtime friend and accomplished biochemist.

# Contents

# Illustrations

*Every science and every inquiry, and similarly every activity and pursuit, is thought to aim at some good.* — Aristotle

# Preface and Acknowledgments

The women whose stories make up this book qualify as scientists because they were trained as such. They used that training in very different ways, as exemplified by Karen Horney and Maria Goeppert Mayer. Some had longer than others to spread their influence; Nettie Stevens died at 50, Alice Hamilton at 101. While most of them did not marry and bear children, some did. I selected them primarily based on their accomplishments, but I also took into account the fields they represented and the interesting aspects of their lives. The book is for the general reader who is interested in American history; it should have special appeal to women.

I am indebted to many for assistance: the archives of Bryn Mawr College, Mount Holyoke College and Wellesley College; G.A. Burchett of Glaxo Wellcome; Dr. Gertrude Elion; Dr. Abbot Gaunt; June Goldblum of the National Academy of Sciences; Dr. Mary Good; Katherine Hayes of the American Institute of Physics; Hollee Haswell at Columbia University; Dr. Katherine Lorbach of the New York City Health and Hospitals Corporation; John McClaughry; Dr. Arthur Pardee; and Dr. Rosalyn Yalow.

Mary Frey came to my rescue by redrawing a photo of which I had only a poor scan.

The staffs of the Peter White Public Library and Northern Michigan University's Lydia M. Olson Library have been most helpful. As usual, I am profoundly grateful to Joanne Whitley, Superiorland Library Cooperative, who never fails to find difficult-to-locate materials.

Moira Davison Reynolds
*Marquette, Michigan*

1

# Introduction

For most of the twentieth century, women had little encouragement to become scientists. There were few role models and mentors; affirmative action was not practiced until the 1980s. Nevertheless, there were women astronomers, zoologists, geneticists and so on; for example, there were women pioneers other than Marie Curie working in the field of radioactivity. The subjects of this book are 23 able and determined American women, each of whom distinguished herself in her respective field.

Cornelia Clapp became professor of zoology at Mount Holyoke College in 1904. (In 1906, there were only 75 female scientists employed by academic institutions in the United States.)

In 1905, Nettie Stevens showed that specific chromosomes determine an individual's sex.

Four years later, Florence Bascom was promoted to the rank of geologist by the United States Geological Survey.

Annie Jump Cannon pursued a career in astronomy from 1896 to 1940, discovering some 300 variable stars and five novas.

After conducting pioneering studies of lead poisoning among pottery workers and painters, physician Alice Hamilton worked for many years for the prevention of occupational disease.

Florence Sabin's research on the lymphatic system brought her membership in the National Academy of Sciences.

Josephine Baker's efforts in public health during the first two decades of this century were responsible for a significant drop in New York City's infant death rate.

Under Mary Rose, Teachers College of Columbia University became a recognized center for the teaching of nutrition.

Karen Horney, a well-trained psychoanalyst, began in the 1920s to disagree with some aspects of Freudian theory. By the 1940s, she had founded institutions that encouraged research into new aspects of psychoanalysis.

Between 1931 and 1968, zoologist Libbie Hyman was engaged in writing an authoritative six-volume work on the invertebrates.

The *Journal of the American Medical Association* in 1945 reported an operation devised by Helen Taussig, a cardiologist, to save the lives of "blue babies."

By the 1950s, modern hospitals throughout the world were using the Apgar score to make a rapid evaluation of the conditions of infants just after delivery. The test was devised by Virginia Apgar, an anesthesiologist.

World War II provided the opportunity for mathematician-physicist Grace Hopper to have a distinguished career in both computer science and the U.S. Navy.

The indiscriminate use of pesticides spurred biologist Rachel Carson to write a warning that changed man's thinking about his environment.

Ruth Sager, a geneticist, discovered in an alga a nonchromosomal gene that governed sensitivity to the drug streptomycin.

Experimental physicist Chien-Shiung Wu became a full professor at Columbia University in 1957. A year later, she was elected to the National Academy of Sciences for experimentally confirming an important hypothesis.

Six American women scientists won Nobel prizes: Gerty Cori in 1947, biochemistry; Maria Goeppert Mayer in 1963, nuclear physics; Rosalyn Yalow in 1977, medical physics; Barbara McClintock in 1983, genetics; Rita Levi-Montalcini in 1986, neurobiology; Gertrude Elion in 1988, synthesis of pharmacological compounds.

By 1980, Mary Good was making a career as an industrial chemist. She received the 1997 Priestly Award, the American Chemical Society's prestigious honor for distinguished services to chemistry.

The stories of these 23 women follow. The importance of their work varies, but each woman contributed to scientific progress in the United States.

# Chapter 1

# Cornelia Clapp
## *Zoologist and Teacher*

*Let nature be your teacher.* — William Wordsworth

Cornelia Clapp devoted much of her professional life to the development of a strong program in zoology at Mount Holyoke College, an institution founded in 1837 to provide what was for its day advanced education for women.

She was born on March 17, 1849, in Montague, Massachusetts, to Richard and Eunice (Slate) Clapp. Three sons and three daughters were born later to the Clapps. Cornelia was of English descent, and her father's family had lived in Montague for several generations. Both parents had been teachers at some time. A successful farmer, Richard Clapp also followed intellectual pursuits.

Cornelia attended local public and private schools. In 1868 she entered Mount Holyoke Seminary, the forerunner of the college. The choice may have been influenced by Cornelia's mother, who was friendly with Fedelia Fiske, a distinguished Mount Holyoke alumna who served as a missionary in Persia. Cornelia graduated after three years' study. During this time, she was impressed by the enthusiasm of Lydia Shattuck, the professor of botany who had been a student of school founder Mary Lyon. Lyon had recognized the importance of science and had succeeded in incorporating key courses into her curriculum.

After a year of teaching Latin to boys in a school in Pennsylvania, in 1872, Clapp began her long academic career at Mount Holyoke — a career that would influence many women scientists of the twentieth century.

Eighteen seventy-three was the year when Grant began his second term, when James Whistler's *Artist's Mother* was unveiled, when Jules Verne's *Around the World in Eighty Days* was published. In the scientific world, *The Origin of the Species* was still controversial; the germ theory of disease was yet to come;

Mendel's work on inheritance was ignored; and although the periodic table of the properties of the elements was available, the structure of the atom was not understood.

Despite being "invited back to teach," Cornelia's subject was not stated. She taught mathematics the first year, then natural history, which would soon be known as zoology. From 1876 to 1891, she was a gymnastics instructor and put together a manual of exercises.

Lydia Shattuck remained an important Mount Holyoke faculty member until she died in 1889. Clapp was generally regarded as her star teacher, as she had been her star pupil. It was probably because of the Shattuck influence that during the summer of 1894, Cornelia was able to attend the Anderson School of Natural History at Penikese Island in Buzzards Bay, Massachusetts. This had been established by Louis Agassiz, the late Swiss American zoologist and geologist who was an exceptionally popular teacher. His philosophy of studying nature, not books, persisted at Penikese, making a deep impression on Cornelia.

Clapp soon introduced an embryology class at Mount Holyoke. Determined to have laboratory science, not just book descriptions, she used a brood hen. She also begged specimens from Mount Holyoke graduates abroad (many were in the mission field). When she received shells, corals and such from them, she compared the latter to specimens at Harvard's Museum of Comparative Zoology to ensure correct identification.

In the summer of 1875, Clapp went with some entomologists to collect insects on a walking trip through the White Mountains of New Hampshire. In 1876, Williston Hall was opened with a special laboratory for zoology, and museum rooms for collections. Over the years, there would be additions of shells, birds, butterflies — even a whale skeleton.

Apparently the college gardener helped when collections of bones were needed; once when Cornelia was away from the campus he wrote to her on a post card:

> The fox on the mountain, he roams at his will,
> The fox in the valley, he lieth there still,
> But the mink in the brook, ah, his spirit has fled,
> And he lies in the box, dismembered and dead.

Two years later, Clapp made a more extensive trip with a group of zoologists led by David Starr Jordan. Starr had studied under Agassiz at Penikese Island and would shortly become head of the department of natural sciences at Indiana University. The party's route was through the South, and members had opportunity to visit the new Johns Hopkins University marine station in Beaufort, South Carolina, as well as the Smithsonian Institution in Washington. They collected fish from creeks and rivers, wading deep into the water.

The South still showed ravages from the Civil War, which made a deep impression on Cornelia. The devastation was always in the back of her mind; it was resurrected later by World War I. Years after that war, a colleague would declare, "Never have I met anyone who had a greater horror of war, a nobler ideal of peace."

In 1879 Clapp spent her first summer abroad. She joined another group led by Jordan, and did much walking in Switzerland. A second such excursion took place in 1886. Eventually she came to know various zoologists in England and throughout Europe. She was faithful in attending pertinent meetings of scientific associations. These contacts outside of Mount Holyoke contributed to her broad grasp of the field.

Cornelia Clapp
(Courtesy Mount Holyoke College Archives and Special Collections, South Hadley, Massachusetts)

Clapp spent a short period of time at the Massachusetts Institute of Technology studying chick embryology under Professor W.T. Sedgwick. In the early 1880s she went to Williams College for five weeks to learn about the earthworm from eminent scientist Edmund Beecher Wilson. He remembered her as "an ardent, enthusiastic and highly intelligent student whom it was a pleasure to teach."

Around this time, she instituted at her alma mater an honor program, but was considered an innovation in her day. To her joy, an annex was added to Williston Hall in 1889, providing more room for zoology. She was firmly behind the transition of female seminary to college, with attendant more advanced courses. That became a reality in the 1890s.

In 1888, Syracuse University had conferred on her the degree of Ph.B, and one year later, the Ph.D. She had qualified for both by examination. In keeping with the improved standards at Mount Holyoke, she took a three-year leave of absence for graduate study at the University of Chicago. (Only 11 years earlier had Helen Magill received a Ph.D. from Boston University, thereby becoming the first woman in the United States to hold that degree.) Clapp's doctoral dissertation on the toadfish was published in 1889 in the *Journal of Morphology*. She disliked writing, and little else of her research was published.

Her long association with the Marine Biological Laboratory in Woods Hole began in the summer of 1888, the year that laboratory opened. She would continue this work until her death in 1934. She was at first a student and investigator, then a lecturer, later a librarian, and finally a trustee. In 1917 she built a home at Woods Hole, where she enjoyed the company of two of her sisters. As time went on, there was a movement to make Woods Hole solely a research institution. Clapp, however, advocated a policy of combining research and teaching and of maintaining close ties with colleges and universities.

Clapp's third European trip in 1903 included study in Naples at its famous biology laboratory. By 1904 she was made professor of zoology at Mount Holyoke College. The first edition of *American Man of Science*, published in 1906, noted her among the nation's 150 most important zoologists.

Although she never married, she was apparently satisfied with her life: She was known to have said, "I have always had the idea if you want to do a thing there is no particular reason why you shouldn't do it."

During a visit to the Far East in 1908-09, Clapp visited many Mount Holyoke alumnae. In 1917, the year after she retired from active teaching, Williston Hall burned. The new Cornelia Clapp Laboratory, a gift from alumnae and friends, was first used in 1921.

After retirement, she and her sisters began to spend winters at Mount Dora, Florida, where she became a leader in church and local affairs. In time she would say, "If anybody had told me that I should have as much pleasure as I have had in these 10 years since I retired, I *never* would have believed it!"

At 85, six months before her death, she joined a parade led by a brass band — part of an alumnae function at Mount Holyoke. She died at her winter home on December 31, 1934. Her ashes were returned to her birthplace for burial.

Cornelia Clapp's character and personality can be glimpsed through written comments made by friends and colleagues. She had a strong religious faith; she was able to adapt to change; she lived in the present, refraining from fretting over the past or worrying about the future; she kept abreast of the events of the day by reading magazines and daily newspapers. High praise came from a male scientist at Woods Hole: "Enthusiasm and loyal devotion, humor, modesty and wisdom combined to make her a unique personality, respected and beloved by all her associates."

After her death, faculty members at her alma mater referred to her adventuring spirit as that "which had made her bring research to Mount Holyoke, at a time when research was little known or encouraged."

Clapp helped build a strong science faculty at a high-ranking institution of higher learning for women. This was important at the time because it encouraged women to consider the study of, for example, biology, in addition to English and other subjects popular at the time.

Today, in an atmosphere where grants are all-important to career advancement and where a "publish-or-perish" philosophy dominates, Cornelia's failure to write up her research would be inexcusable. In her day, her accomplishments as a teacher were recognized and appreciated.

# Chapter 2

# Nettie Stevens
## *Researcher in Cytology*

*Male and female created he them.* — Genesis 1:27

Bryn Mawr College had much influence on the professional life of Nettie Stevens. Unlike Cornelia Clapp, she was relatively free from teaching obligations and thus able to pursue her research interests. Her most important finding demonstrated the relationship between two sets of sex chromosomes and the determination of sex.

Nettie Maria Stevens was born July 7, 1861, in Cavendish, Vermont, to Ephriam Stevens and Julia (Adams) Stevens. Little is known of the parents except that they were New Englanders; that Ephriam was a native of Chelmsford, Massachusetts, and an industrious carpenter; and that Julia died in 1863. Nettie and her sister were cared for by a stepmother, the former Ellen Thompson.

The family moved to Westford, Massachusetts, where by 1875 Ephriam had accumulated considerable property. Nettie went to public and private schools, graduating from Westport Academy in 1880. After a stint as a high school teacher, she attended Westfield State Normal School in Massachusetts from 1881 to 1883. There she distinguished herself as an excellent student. She also participated in debates and played the piano, still managing to complete the course in record time. Nettie pursued a highly successful teaching career for some years, and for a short period in her life worked at the free library in Chelmsford. There are few clues to the understanding of her personality.

Enrolling at Stanford University in 1896, she obtained both B.A. and M.A. degrees from that California institution. Her field was biology with an emphasis on cytology, the branch that deals with the microscopic appearance and structure of cells. While studying at Stanford, she spent four summers at the Hopkins Seaside Laboratory in Pacific Grove, California.

9

The year 1900 saw Stevens accepted at Bryn Mawr College in Pennsylvania as a candidate for the Ph.D. program. Founded by the Society of Friends and opened in 1885, Bryn Mawr was one of the first women's colleges to offer graduate degrees. Since her field was cytology, the choice was fortunate. Edmund Beecher Wilson, under whom Cornelia Clapp had studied at Williams College, was Bryn Mawr's first biology professor. After he left for Columbia University in 1891, he was succeeded by Thomas Hunt Morgan, a future Nobel laureate. Both men were able and influential in the fields of genetics and cytology.

Stevens received a fellowship that enabled her to spend her second predoctoral year at the Zoological Station in Naples, Italy, and at the Zoological Institute of the University of Würzburg, Germany. At the latter, she studied under Theodor Boveri, who was interested in chromosomes. (She would return to Würzburg for additional study from 1908 to 1909.) By 1903, when Nettie completed the Ph.D. requirements, she had published several papers dealing with regeneration.

In the summer of 1903, Stevens applied to the Carnegie Institute for a fellowship to "continue research work instead of teaching next year." She stated that her interest was in the microscopic study of the structure of factors related to Mendel's law.

At that time knowledge about genetics was very limited. Chromosomes, appearing under the microscope as rod shaped structures in the cell, had been observed for many years, but their significance was not known. It was recognized that each species had a specific number of chromosomes, and that in the nuclei of egg and sperm cells a special stepwise process of cell division (meiosis) halved the chromosome number so that their union produced a new individual with the species-specific number of chromosomes. Gregor Mendel's work, published in 1866, was largely ignored until its rediscovery in 1900. Mendel had shown that heredity characteristics were determined by particulate factors, now called genes, for which chromosomes were vehicles; also that the transmission of one pair of factors was independent of the transmission of another pair. From this, the theory was advanced that one number of a pair of chromosomes was of maternal origin, the other of paternal origin. This theory is now fact, but not all biologists at that time were convinced that chromosomes were linked to sex determination. Experimental proof was needed.

In 1903 W.S. Sutton pointed out an association between Mendel's factors and chromosomes. A definite stimulus to Stevens' research was the suggestion by C.E. McClung that an "accessory" chromosome, known as the X chromosome, determined maleness. Although this suggestion was later proven incorrect — it is the Y chromosome that determines maleness — the idea spurred Nettie's interest, already aroused by her work with Boveri.

Her application for a fellowship was supported by Morgan. He noted her independent and original mind and that she "does thoroughly whatever she undertakes." Wilson, who at that time maintained close ties with Morgan and Bryn Mawr, wrote: "I know Miss Stevens' work well, and it is of a very independent and admirable character from every point of view. I consider her not only the best of the women investigators but one whose work will hold its own with that of any of the men of the same degree of advancement."

**Nettie Stevens**
**(Courtesy Bryn Mawr College Archives)**

The fellowship she sought was granted, allowing Stevens to remain at Bryn Mawr as research fellow in biology for the year 1904-05. She continued to be affiliated with the college, acting as an associate in experimental morphology until she died in 1912. After Stevens' death, Morgan noted the liberality of Bryn Mawr College, in creating for her a research position. In the same article, he made it clear that her native ability and devotion to work were the prime factors in her accomplishments.

Between 1901 and 1912, Stevens published more than 38 papers on cytology and experimental physiology. Sturtevant's *A History of Genetics*, published in 1965, notes her contribution to science. Referring to McClung's interpretation as "reverse of the true one," he wrote:

> The correct relation was shown in 1905 for a beetle (Tenebrio) by Stevens; in this case there was also a Y present, smaller than the X, and she showed clearly that the female is XX, the male XY. This result was immediately confirmed by Wilson (also in 1905) for Hemiptera and was soon shown for Orthoptera, Diptera, Homoptera Myriapoda, and with less certainty, for various kinds of animals.

Some authorities believe that Wilson submitted his work for publication before Stevens did, but that he failed to get credit because he wrote: "great, if not insuperable, difficulties are encountered by any form of assumption that these chromosomes [sex chromosomes] are specific male or female determinants." (Some scientists attributed the differences in the sexes to environmental, rather than chromosomal, factors.)

In contrast, Stevens concluded: "this seems to be a clear case of sex determination, not by an accessory chromosome, but by a definite difference in the character of the elements of one pair of chromosomes of the spermatocytes of the first order, the spermatozoa which contain the small chromosome determining the male sex, while those that contain 10 chromosomes of equal size determine the female sex."

For the next six years, Stevens extended her work in the subject over a wide field. According to Morgan, an extensive study was necessary, for the profound significance of the results was not generally appreciated; in fact, many cytologists assumed a skeptical or even antagonistic attitude towards the new discovery.

Stevens did not live long enough to gain fame — she died of cancer of the breast when she was 50. However, her experimental work began the quest to find out exactly how sex is determined.

Some 66 years after Nettie's death, Stephen Brush wrote:

> neither Stevens nor Wilson is now given adequate recognition by writers of texts and popular works on biology; most of the credit for the establishment of modern genetics usually goes to Thomas Hunt Morgan (1866-1945), who would not accept the chromosome theory until several years after the work of Stevens and Wilson had been published.
>
> Those who seek outstanding female scientists to inspire the next generation of talented women to follow scientific careers seem to have overlooked Nettie Stevens.

Stevens' name has unfortunately been overlooked; it (and that of Wilson, but not of Morgan) is absent from the 1990 edition of *Molecular Cell Biology*, somehow forgotten amongst the amazing progress made in genetics since the middle of the twentieth century.

# Chapter 3

# Florence Bascom
## *Geologist and Teacher*

*One generation passeth away, and another generation cometh,*
*but the earth abideth for ever.* — Ecclesiastes 1:4

Florence Bascom was a competent geologist and teacher, but her unique contribution was the demonstration that productive collaboration was possible between academic geology and its practice in government.

She was born on July 14, 1862, in Williamstown, Massachusetts, to John and Emma (Curtiss) Bascom and was the youngest of six children; three of the latter died before reaching adulthood. Both parents, with New England roots, exhibited the pioneer spirit. At the same time, they had a liberal outlook. John Bascom was well-educated and involved in academe. His wife was learned and refined and very interested in the advancement of women.

A serious and studious child, Florence liked to spend time with her father. She attributed to him her interest in the outdoor world. Her love and respect for him was an integral part of her life.

When she was 12, the family moved to Madison, Wisconsin, when John Bascom became the president of the University of Wisconsin. One high school report card dated 1877 revealed that Florence had received no grade below 95 percent. According to a newspaper account of the school's graduation ceremonies, Miss Florence Bascom, in reading an essay, "lisped quite prettily, thus adding a charm to the interest of her delivery, which was otherwise expressive and by no means monotonous." The young lady graduates were "in many cases elaborately dressed, the prevailing mode being muslin and silk dresses, with white gloves and throat trimmings of smilax and rosebuds, and festoons of the former, mingled with lace."

Late in life, Florence wrote some reminiscences of her youth spent in Madison. She noted the board sidewalk leading to the president's house; she also confessed responsibility for, at a later date, felling a distinguished geologist when she (Florence) stepped upon a loose board in such a sidewalk. She recalled a time when occasionally an incoming freshman sent his luggage to the president's home pending a permanent location; a time when the influences of literary societies was great; a time when the inadequate university gymnasium was used by men exclusively.

When John Bascom assumed the presidency of the University of Wisconsin, women were being admitted as regular students. However, men and women were not permitted to use the library on the same day, and if a classroom lacked seats to accommodate all registered students, males in nearly all cases had preference. John Bascom's aim was to provide equal educational opportunities for women; he also supported a more flexible curriculum and research opportunities for the faculty.

Florence enrolled at her father's institution, where she received a somewhat broad-based education; in 1882, she was awarded two bachelor degrees — in literature and the arts. (Curiously, she knew little about music — which her father considered frivolous.) By 1894 Bascom had received a third bachelor's degree from the University of Wisconsin, this one in science.

Apparently she spent the late summer and early fall months of 1882 in travel to the Dakota Territory, where she observed much of the region's Indian culture.

A postgraduate year was spent at the Hampton Institute in Virginia, where she taught without pay. Hampton had opened in 1868 and was one of the first colleges for blacks; it also pioneered in the education of Native Americans. Samuel Chapman Armstrong, its founder, was known and admired by John Bascom.

On returning to Madison, Bascom began work for her master's degree in geology. Her interest in the subject had been heightened by a visit with her father to Mammoth Cave in Kentucky. The curriculum for the science degree had provided her with the necessary basic background.

At the time, geology was influenced by the work of Charles Lyell, the British geologist who had propounded the idea of uniformitarianism as opposed to catastrophism. The former view, originally offered by James Hulton, held that contemporary processes produced effects on the earth in the same way through the ages, and with about the same intensity; and that there was a delicate balance between biologic and geologic processes. The work of Lyell and Darwin was threatening to some who held strong religious convictions. The microscopic study of rocks and minerals was just beginning in the United States, being more advanced in Germany.

Bascom's special interests were structural geology and petrography. The latter involves the description and systematic classification of rocks. Working under the direction of Charles Van Hise, she investigated the sheet gobbros (granular igneous rocks rich in magnesium) of Lake Superior. Her master of arts degree was awarded in 1887 by the University of Wisconsin.

That year, President Bascom left Madison, returning to the faculty of Williams College in Massachusetts. Florence moved with her family and for a short time taught Greek and physical geography at the local high school. In her spare time she made watercolor paintings and charcoal drawings.

On obtaining a position at Rockford College in Illinois, she taught geology and chemistry for two years. At this time, she decided to obtain her Ph.D. in geology and devote her professional life to that subject. She appeared to have rejected marriage as part of her life. (In old age, she declared that her association with her father gratified all she wanted or needed so far as men were concerned.)

**Florence Bascom**
**(Courtesy Bryn Mawr College Archives)**

Recommended by her professors at Wisconsin, Bascom entered the graduate school of Johns Hopkins University in 1889. George Huntington Williams, who brought to Hopkins new ideas from Heidelberg, Germany, supervised her program. Her thesis, of course, required extensive field work — sometimes with other geologists, sometimes alone. She was chased by bulls, was called "the Stone Lady," and often was cursed at for trespassing. Unmoved, she used the microscope and other means to show that, contrary to earlier views, the ancient pre–Cambrian rocks of Maryland's South Mountain were altered volcanic rather than sedimentary rock.

Although Bascom had been admitted to graduate study, she had no assurance that a woman would be granted a degree. However, six months before graduation, she received that assurance from the president of Johns Hopkins University. In June 1893 she became the first female recipient of a Ph.D. from that institution.

That year, *The Milwaukee Journal* described Florence as a blond, of medium height, not a beauty, but a person with pleasing features — a woman apparently engrossed in her studies and an ardent advocate of women's rights.

For the next two years, she was an assistant to Edward Orton, the professor of geology at Ohio State University in Columbus. Orton, incidentally, was an acquaintance of John Bascom and another person who had aroused Florence's interest in the field of geology.

In 1893, at the age of 33, Bascom began her long association with Bryn Mawr College. It was three years before Florence could establish a geology department. At first, geology was a sort of elective in the departments of biology and chemistry. At one point, she refused reappointment as associate, insisting on and winning the title of associate professor.

Building the research-oriented department that she envisioned was no easy task. There was limited space, no library of works related to geology, no specimens, no laboratory equipment, and a very limited budget. But the determined professor prevailed. By the first decade of the twentieth century, her department was receiving the recognition due a first-class facility: There was now an associate with expertise in fields other than Florence's, and there were graduate students from both the United States and abroad.

Bascom herself was promoted to the rank of full professor. In 1894 she had been elected a fellow of the Geological Society of America, the first woman so honored. In 1897 she attended the International Geological Congress in St. Petersburg. On that occasion, a male colleague noted that she was the one woman in the world who had a right to be there. In later years she went to similar events in Mexico, Canada, Finland, Greenland and Washington, D.C. She took a sabbatical leave in 1906 to study in Heidelberg, Germany, with Victor Goldschmidt, a leading crystallographer. Thanks to this experience, she was better able to promote optical crystallography in the United States.

Another important contact was the United States Geological Survey, organized in 1879 under the Department of the Interior. With her appointment in 1896 as assistant geologist, she became the first female member. To put that into perspective, in 1896 Henri Becquerel discovered radioactivity, leading to important advances in geology and other branches of science.

The U.S. Geological Survey was furnishing geologic maps for every square mile in the public domain. Soon promoted to geologist, Bascom was assigned to study the Mid-Atlantic Piedmont of the Appalachians, a large area of crystalline rocks between the Susquehanna and Delaware rivers in Southeastern Pennsylvania and adjoining states. This project occupied her for many years. In the summer she collected specimens, making notes about them. In the winter, after studying thin sections prepared for the petrographic microscope, she wrote up results. The findings were published in several major geologic folios.

Aside from U.S.G.S. work, Bascom's own research was published between 1893 and 1938 in the form of some 40 articles. By 1937, 12 women were members of the Geological Society of America, several of whom had studied under Florence. She retired from Bryn Mawr in 1928.

Bascom spent some of her retirement at an old farmhouse named

Topping in the Berkshire Hills of Massachusetts, but she was in Washington for several winters to complete her work with the U.S.G.S. She retired permanently to Topping in 1940.

Florence was apparently rather reserved, but a little is known about her personality from observations by friends and colleagues. A lover of animals, especially dogs and horses, she worked as an advocate for their care and for the protection of wildlife; she enjoyed riding a horse given her by an uncle, and later its colt; she loved jewelry made of gems and of semiprecious stones; she was generous with money, at times contributing to the support of a brother; she wore elegant clothes when the occasion demanded, yet her sensible and comfortable attire for field work occasionally shocked Victorian-minded acquaintances; she even cut her hair just as soon as she left Bryn Mawr; she was a feminist but concentrated on gaining rights by demonstrating her ability. She once wrote, "The selection of work in which one delights, and a diligent adherence to it, are main ingredients of success."

During the last years of her life, her memory failed. She died in 1945 at age 82 in Massachusetts' Northampton State Hospital.

Florence Bascom — a progressive woman — would surely be intrigued to know that one goal of NASA's Mars Mission is to analyze the composition of Martian rocks.

# Chapter 4

# Annie Jump Cannon
## *Astronomer*

*He telleth the number of stars; he calleth them all by names.*
— Psalms 147:4.

Annie Jump Cannon was a full-time researcher. Like Nettie Stevens, she had no arduous teaching obligations. An expert in stellar classification by means of photographic spectra, she spent more than four decades in very careful cataloguing of hundreds of thousands of stars.

Annie was born on December 11, 1863, in Dover, Delaware, to Wilson Lee Cannon and Mary Elizabeth (Jump) Cannon, his second wife. Annie's siblings included two younger brothers, an older brother and three older half-sisters. Of Scottish descent, Wilson Cannon was a prosperous merchant and former shipbuilder. He was lieutenant governor of Delaware when the issue of secession was debated. Although he was a Democrat, he voted with the Republicans. His act of conscience broke a tie vote and ensured that Delaware would remain in the Union; it also cost him the friendship of some who had helped him politically. Mrs. Cannon's roots went back to seventeenth century Maryland.

Annie spent a seemingly happy childhood in a cultured family. She attended public schools and at 16 graduated from Wilmington Conference Academy in Dover. Her mother had some knowledge of astronomy and, while Annie was still a child, interested her in the subject. The Cannons' large white house had a roof that could be approached from a trap door in the attic. Thus it served as an observatory, and here young Annie learned about constellations, using candlelight to record her observations. Her father, incidentally, had little interest in astronomy.

Annie's intellectual ability impressed her teachers at the academy to the extent that they suggested to Wilson Cannon that his daughter would profit

**Annie Jump Cannon**
**(Courtesy Harvard College Observatory)**

from a college education. After a trip north to investigate various institutions, he chose Wellesley College in Massachusetts.

His daughter benefited from the choice. Wellesley, opened in 1875, was the first women's college with scientific laboratories. Here Annie learned from Professor Sarah F. Whiting, who had studied physics at the Massachusetts Institute of Technology and who had, with difficulty, acquired the laboratory equipment deemed necessary to teach physics at the new institution. Whiting was told by a male physicist that he had never dreamed of discussing the Wheatstone bridge (which measured electrical resistances) with a lady. From the Wellesley professor the young student from Delaware developed an interest in spectroscopy — an interest that would play a major role in her life.

Spectroscopy was one of the underlying principles used in the study of the stars. When photographic film became available, it was possible to make records of the spectra of various celestial bodies by using a telescope, a spectrometer, and a camera.

After graduation from Wellesley in 1884, Annie lived at home for many years, with no contact with spectroscopy and other scientific proceedures.

One summer she went to Europe, returning with interesting photographs. A beautiful woman, she attracted men but did not marry.

After Mrs. Cannon's death in 1893, Annie returned to Wellesley for a year of postgraduate study — again under Sarah Whiting's direction. Then she enrolled at Radcliffe College in Cambridge, Massachusetts, as a special student in astronomy. While at Radcliffe, she met Edward Pickering, the director of the Harvard College Observatory in Cambridge (now part of the Harvard-Smithsonian Center for Astrophysics). Receptive to the employment of women, he offered Cannon a position.

Pickering was directing a project set up to record, classify and catalogue the spectra of all stars, including those with very low magnitudes of brightness. In 1879, he had hired his housekeeper, Williamina Fleming, to assist on a temporary basis. She proved so competent that after two years she was made a permanent member of Pickering's staff. Mrs. Fleming had made numerous improvements in Pickering's original system; Cannon's charge was to make additional improvements and simplifications. This she would do over the next 45 years. Under her, the classification system became flexible and more usable. Eighteen ninety-six, the year when Annie first worked at the Harvard Observatory, was also the year that William McKinley was elected the twenty-fifth president and that the first Nobel Prizes were awarded according to the terms of the will of Alfred Nobel, the Swedish chemist and inventor.

Cannon approached her work with intelligence, interest and, especially, patience. She was fortunate in having unusual powers of observation. In 1900, when she became responsible for the card catalogue of the literature on variable stars, it contained 14,000 cards; when she died, there were some 250,000 references.

After Mrs. Fleming's death in 1911, Cannon became curator of astronomical photographs. This required her to examine the quality of all plates taken between 1911 and 1938. During her tenure, the observatory plate collection grew from some 200,000 to about 500,000. No doubt her constant presence was advantageous to the progress.

Her effort was reflected in *The Henry Draper Catalogue* (1918–24) and *The Henry Draper Extension* (1925-49) — both in use today. The catalogue, named in memory of an American pioneer in stellar spectroscopy and financed by his widow, gives the spectral classification and the visual and photographic magnitudes of stars in all parts of the sky, together with positions sufficiently accurate for their identification. Harlow Shapley, the eminent astronomer who succeeded Pickering in 1921, referred to Annie's contribution to astronomy as "a structure that probably will never be duplicated in kind or extent by a single individual."

In the course of her work, Cannon discovered many relatively rare stars, including about 300 variable stars and five novas — stars that brighten intensely and then gradually diminish.

She also became a successful lecturer. She loved to travel, attending regularly the triennial meetings of the International Astronomical Union held in such cities as Paris, Cambridge, Stockholm and London. In 1922 she spent some months at Harvard's observatory in the Peruvian Andes.

Some things are known of her personal life. She liked to entertain and kept in touch with her Wellesley friends. Being very fond of children, she instituted an annual Easter egg rolling contest for the children of observatory personnel. She supported female suffrage and was disappointed when women failed to vote. She followed her father by remaining a Republican. A prized possession in her Cambridge home called "Star Cottage" was a candelabra whose prisms had fascinated her as a youth in Dover. In 1933 she established the Annie J. Cannon Prize, to be awarded every third year to an outstanding woman astronomer; she specified that the prize be a brooch which the recipient could use, rather than a ceremonial medal.

For her work, Annie Jump Cannon received many honors, the highest, perhaps, being honorary membership in the Royal Astronomical Society. (Women were not accepted as regular members.) Not possessing an earned doctorate, she received four honorary degrees, including Doctor of Science from Oxford.

In middle age, she suffered from severe deafness. Nevertheless, she continued to work until the year of her death. She died of heart failure and arteriosclerosis in 1941 at the age of 77.

Annie Jump Cannon had enthusiasm, great perseverance and the ability to deal with detail — all characteristics useful to a scientist and valued today. She came close to telling the number of the stars and calling them by their names, feats the psalmist attributed to God.

In a posthumous tribute to his colleague, Shapley said this:

> She must be classed among a group of pioneer women scientists. Most of her fellow pioneers were largely engaged in educational projects; she was nearly unique by being engaged on the creative side of the great process of understanding. She was engaged in scientific researches in a specialized field. Her persistent activity has been a guiding light to women scholars. Her success has been their inspiration.

Today, the Annie Jump Cannon Award in Astronomy, given by the American Association of University Women in conjunction with the American Astronomical Society, annually recognizes a woman astronomer pursuing significant postdoctoral research in astronomy while in the early stages of her career.

# Chapter 5

# Alice Hamilton
## *Pioneer Industrial Physician*

*To protect workers in their inalienable rights to a higher and better life; to protect them not only as equals before the law, but also in their health.* — Samuel Gompers, 1898

Alice Hamilton established the practice of industrial medicine in the United States. Her interest in the field was spurred by a strong social consciousness. Much is known about her life: Her autobiography gives one picture, while her letters, as presented in Sicherman's *Alice Hamilton: A Life in Letters,* yield additional insight.

Alice Hamilton was born on February 27, 1869, in New York City to Montgomery and Gertrude (Pond) Hamilton, the second of five children. Montgomery Hamilton, whose forebears were Scottish and Irish, was well-educated. He was not a successful businessman, living mainly on inherited money. He also drank to excess. His wife, of English and Dutch extraction, was not only well-educated, but had a liberal outlook that she imparted to Alice. The latter remembered her mother as free from the Victorian prudery considered essential to a lady — she even discussed sex problems; above all, to Gertrude Hamilton, personal liberty was the most precious thing in life.

When Alice was six weeks old, her mother returned with her to Fort Wayne, Indiana, the home of three generations of Hamiltons. Here the future physician enjoyed a childhood of privilege and comfort with siblings and cousins. Alice was educated at home because her mother objected to the long hours required by the public schools; her father did not approve of the curriculum. The Hamilton children were taught languages, literature, history and a smattering of mathematics. (Montgomery taught Latin, Gertrude beginning French. The servants started them in German, and later a Lutheran schoolteacher instructed them in that language.) It was also parental teaching that made them familiar with the Bible. This schooling appeared to serve their needs—for example, Alice, later in life, had no trouble in conversing with Germans and Frenchmen. Following Hamilton tradition, Alice, when she was 17, attended Miss Porter's School in Farmington, Connecticut, for two years. Summers were spent at first in West Virginia, and then for many years at Michigan's Mackinac Island, where the family owned a cottage. Alice's vivid memories include nights spent in an open boat , or on the mainland's shore, when Montgomery would take his children with him on a fishing trip. When she was older, Alice rode a bike.

After Miss Porter's School, Edith, the oldest sister, and Alice decided they must be prepared to earn their own living because the family finances were much diminished. They considered teaching, nursing and medicine. Edith chose

**Alice Hamilton**
**(Courtesy Library of Congress)**

the first and Alice the last. Alice's decision was made because as a physician she could go anywhere, work independently and be of service.

Her family, in general, were not enthusiastic about her becoming a doctor. But they did not voice strong opposition. However, Agnes Hamilton, the cousin to whom Alice remained very close and to whom she would reveal herself in numerous letters, encouraged her to study medicine.

Alice's immediate task was to prepare herself academically, and this she began by studying physics and chemistry with a high school teacher. She was deficient in biology as well. After classes at Fort Wayne College of Medicine, she entered the University of Michigan Medical School in March 1892, graduating in June the following year. She was one of 14 women in a class of 47. The period at Ann Arbor proved beneficial—the University of Michigan offered one of the best medical programs in the country, and the novelty of being emancipated from a protective family environment appealed to Alice.

Having decided against clinical practice, Hamilton intended to specialize in bacteriology and pathology. However, she took the advice of one of her professors to do a hospital internship; he believed that otherwise she risked being too one-sided.

Hamilton spent two months as an intern in the Hospital for Women and

Children in Minneapolis, then nine months in the New England Hospital for Women and Children in Boston. Her service at the latter involved night calls to slum areas and even to brothels. Alice's correspondence with Agnes during this period shows that her experiences with poor and often uneducated people made her realize that they could possess sterling qualities she had not suspected. With many people unemployed, she had opportunity to make referrals to various charities. She wrote that as her work became more associated with these charities, it became more "delightful." She resigned her internship in May 1894, presumably because she was needed at home.

After caring for her sister Margaret, who had suffered an accident, Alice returned to Ann Arbor early in 1895 to obtain experience in bacteriology. Her professors advised her that Germany was the place to perfect knowledge of bacteriology and pathology. An opportunity offered itself since Edith had a fellowship from Bryn Mawr to study classics abroad.

That fall, the sisters sailed for Germany, where as foreigners they had been permitted to study at Leipzig and Munich. (At that time, some universities in Europe and the United States allowed women to enroll for study, but without guarantee of a degree — the situation that Florence Bascom encountered at Johns Hopkins.)

The year abroad did not add greatly to Hamilton's professional knowledge. It did, though, make her familiar with the fact that in Germany, women were considered inferior. "It was a man's world, in every sense," she wrote, "and at the top was the army, adored and feared by the common man." On the positive side, she developed an affection for the ordinary people of the country.

In 1896 Hamilton began a year at Johns Hopkins Medical School in Baltimore, where Edith became head of the Bryn Mawr School. At Hopkins Alice worked chiefly with Simon Flexner, then a young pathologist destined to become a personage in American medicine. She also knew luminaries William Welch and William Osler, who urged her to accept a position to teach pathology at the Chicago Woman's Medical School, at the time part of Northwestern University's medical school.

At last Hamilton would be earning a living; there would be opportunity to do independent research and to have a four-month vacation every year. More important to her future, she hoped to live at Jane Addams' Hull House or another settlement. After a summer at Mackinac, she went to Chicago, where Jane Addams had found room for her in Hull House.

After having heard the renowned social worker speak in Fort Wayne's Methodist Church, Hamilton dreamed of living at Hull House. She had had little or no exposure to poverty and its results, and was anxious to become familiar with this different world. She was having doubts about her life: "I had a conviction that professional life, teaching pathology, and carrying on research would never satisfy me. I must make for myself a life full of human interest," she wrote.

Opened in 1889 in Chicago's west side, Hull House served as a community center for the neighborhood poor and a nucleus for social reform activities. Educated and cultured people lived in a slum area as neighbors of those less fortunate, most of whom were Italians, Irish, Bohemians, Poles and Greeks. Jane Addams considered Hull House a bridge between the classes — an institute of mutual benefit to both well-to-do and poor. The residents were expected to do volunteer work in addition to paying for room and board. Alice's obligation was to run a well-baby clinic. In return, she learned, for example, that "education and culture have little to do with real wisdom, the wisdom that comes from life experience." She soon saw "how deep and fundamental are the inequalities in our democratic country."

Hamilton would live at Hull House for 22 years. Afterwards, she returned each year for several months until Jane Addams died in 1935. Over the years, she met some very prominent liberals and always found intellectual stimulation there. At the same time, during her early years at Hull House, she felt somewhat useless and found the demands of settlement work excessive. Perhaps this was because her professional work was proving somewhat onerous.

In her new position, she was handicapped by lack of specimens with which to teach. She had to obtain them from Rush Medical College at first, later from autopsies done at Cook County Hospital. She began to despair of losing her interest in research. To add to her consternation at the time, her sister Norah, an artist, had a serious mental breakdown.

When Rush Medical School began to admit women in 1902, the school where Hamilton was teaching closed. Not invited to Rush, she became a researcher under Ludwig Hektoen at the newly created Memorial Institute for Infectious Diseases. She valued the training she received there and later at the Pasteur Institute in Paris, but found that as time went by, she was not absorbed by the life of a laboratory researcher. She decided she would never make her mark in bacteriology.

Life at Hull House had made her keenly aware of how the other half lived: She was now an advocate of fair labor practices, birth control and woman suffrage; she had some leanings towards socialism and was becoming a pacifist. She had also gained a familiarity with the American legal system. While her interest in science waned temporarily, social concerns were occupying much of her energy.

Around 1907 she became interested in industrial diseases. She read a muckraking article by a Chicago settlement worker and then *Dangerous Trades* by a British investigator named Thomas Oliver. These writings stimulated her to read everything she could find on dangers to industrial workers, and what could be done to protect them. She found that in Europe industrial medicine was a recognized medical science. In the United States, however, it did not exist. The implication was that the conditions of American workers were beyond reproach. Alice's familiarity with the Chicago slums made her skeptical; to back up her disbelief, she soon learned that American workers in the match industry suffered from "phossy jaw," a bone necrosis to which the mandible was especially susceptible. The condition was caused by the white or yellow phosphorus then used in the manufacturing of matches. In 1908 Hamilton expressed some of her concerns in an article for *Charities and the Cause.*

Charles Henderson, a professor of sociology at the University of Chicago, was pressing for the type of sickness insurance he had seen in Germany. He urged Charles Deneen, the reform governor of Illinois, to appoint an Occupational Disease Commission. Through Henderson, Hamilton was made a member. During 1910, a survey of the state's industrial poisons was to be conducted. Hamilton was made medical director of the project, assisted by young doctors, medical students and social workers. She was to concentrate on the effects of lead, long known to be an industrial poison. The Illinois survey provided her, at the age of 41, what she had been looking for — an opportunity to use her scientific knowledge and training to benefit social conditions. It was a landmark in her life.

In 1910, there was no control over health and safety conditions in the workplace. (At an international conference on occupational accidents and diseases, held in Brussels, a member of the Belgian Labor Department noted: "It is well known that there is no industrial hygiene in the United States.") Immigrants were inclined to accept existing conditions without protest. Lead poisoning was caused by compounds of lead that entered the body by respiration or ingestion. It could be acute, but more often was chronic, brought about by continuous exposure. The symptoms were the appearance of a blue line on the gums, weakness, anemia, colic, alternating constipation and diarrhea, and paralysis of the wrists and ankles. Massive exposure caused brain damage and death.

The commission had to find actual cases. This entailed reading hospital records, interviewing sick workers, investigating rumors, and speaking with labor leaders and doctors and druggists in work areas. According to Hamilton, the exploration of an unknown field was pioneering, exciting and rewarding work. She had much to learn; for instance, the details of certain manufacturing processes were new to her. From the outset, she was convinced, and correctly so, that lead dust and lead fumes were the culprits. The prevailing view was that lead intoxication took place because a worker did not wash his hands and scrub his nails, thereby allowing entrance to the digestive tract.

The survey identified 77 lead-using industrial processes and 578 cases of lead poisoning. Hamilton was especially proud of her discovery that there was lead in the enamel paint used to make bathtubs — a fact not noted in the literature.

Governor Deneen received the commission's report in January 1911.

Several months later, Illinois passed an occupational disease law. Five other states did likewise before the year ended. The Illinois statute, however, did not provide compensation.

In 1911 Hamilton began a federal survey to cover all states. It was similar to the Illinois survey, investigating the lead trades first. As an employee of the United States Bureau of Labor (later Department), she was given complete independence, but it was understood that her entering any establishment was dependent on the courtesy of the employer. Alice welcomed the move from the laboratory, to which she never returned. She wrote later that she never doubted the wisdom of her giving up laboratory research to devote herself to work that was scientific in part, but human and practical in greater measure.

By 1916 Hamilton was regarded as the leading authority on lead poisoning. Her surveys, which included rubber and munitions plants, exemplified careful documentation. To improve conditions for the workers, she appealed to the better nature of the employers to institute the safety or preventative measures she suggested. She found that often ignorance had been behind deplorable practices, and that with knowledge sometimes came cooperation on the part of those in authority. She had varied roles: medical investigator, advocate for the laborer, and promoter of good health. For fellow physicians, she was a disciple of a new branch of medicine.

The work involved the writing of numerous letters, which she often typed herself. (Her personal correspondence also occupied much of her time.) She did not remain behind a desk in Washington, but traveled about the nation to understand conditions firsthand. Her investigations involved entering mines, factories and the like, often in remote locations. With persistence she conducted detailed and accurate fact finding, then used the facts that she had obtained to further understanding and advocate legislation.

She apparently enjoyed the independence the situation gave her: She was able to return to Hull House and continue the intimate contact she had always shared with her family members. In 1916 she and Margaret purchased a house in Hadlyme, Connecticut, which afforded them more and more pleasure as the years passed. Their brother married, but none of the Hamilton sisters did. As to Alice's bachelorhood, in a letter written in 1896 to her cousin Agnes, she noted, that at the time, girls could choose between an independent life of celibacy or a life devoted to childbearing, and implied that she did not approve of mixing a career with marriage. Her work in industrial medicine and her family contacts seemed to have provided her with a satisfying life.

World War I had a profound effect on Alice. In 1915, with the United States still neutral, Jane Addams headed a delegation of some 50 Americans to an international congress of women held at The Hague. Hamilton accompanied Addams, but not as an official delegate. The hope was to form a conference of men from the neutral nations, which would be an agency of continuous mediation for the settlement of war. Despite many efforts, it failed. According to Hamilton: "Miss Addams and [suffrage leader and pacifist] Dr. [Aletta] Jacobs made a purely human appeal based on the cruelty and futility of war, protesting as women against the suffering, the waste of life, and urging that at least an attempt be made to bring about, through non-violent discussion, adjustment of the quarrels which had given rise to the war."

The war affected Hamilton professionally also. Even before the United States declared war in 1917, high explosives — for example, shells and mines — were needed for the Allies. Involved was the manufacturing of such compounds as picric acid, dinitrobenzene, trinitrotoluene and mercuric fulminate. Since the location of the plants was kept secret, Alice had to play detective to find their whereabouts. She reported 2,432 cases of occupational poisoning found by May 1917, but she had difficulty in making improvements. In 1919, through Samuel Gompers, there was finally a code, though not mandatory, to protect TNT workers. However, the wartime industrial hazards did arouse the interest of physicians: Articles and medical journals discussed new poisons and methods of prevention. As Hamilton wrote, industrial medicine had at last become respectable, and the employers had changed their attitude — the large turnover in labor experienced in the hazardous wartime industries was not efficient.

Hamilton had become a pacifist. She did not suffer great persecution, but anyone with such views was often considered pro–German, anti–American, or even dangerous. Returning to Europe in 1919 for a peace congress meeting in Zurich, she was shocked by the starvation of children, brought about by the postwar blockade as a means to force Germany into accepting the terms of the Versailles Treaty. Women such as herself, Jane Addams, Lillian Wald and Jeannette Rankin believed that infants and children should not be paying for the atrocities of the German government. Hamilton refused to be intimidated by influential persons who thought that Germany should be punished at any cost. She expressed her admiration for the Quakers and helped raise money for their relief efforts.

David Edsall, dean of Harvard Medical School, had a strong interest in industrial medicine. After hearing Hamilton deliver three guest lectures at Harvard, he invited her to join the faculty for six months of each year. He informed President Lowell that she was much superior to any man they knew of for such a position.

Her appointment began in the fall of 1919, but it was not until the beginning of the Harding administration (1921) that she first severed her Washington connections — there were important studies to be completed, for example, on benzene. During the war, she had become interested in this compound and was anxious to demonstrate its danger, which was little recognized at that time in the United States.

For 15 years, Hamilton's Boston home was that of Amory and Katherine

Bowditch Codman, with whom she had much in common. Besides having similar intellectual interests and social concerns, the three enjoyed outdoor life. Between 1921 and 1927, they followed the Sacco-Vanzetti case. Along with her friend jurist Felix Frankfurter and many others, Alice believed that these two Italian anarchists had been convicted of murder because of their beliefs rather than firm evidence. Hamilton was involved in a futile, eleventh-hour appeal to Massachusetts Governor Alvan T. Fuller. Consistent with this, she was known to assist aliens who held subversive views. Prohibition was an issue of the day, but Alice did not support it because personal liberty was involved.

In 1923, she undertook to study the mercury-producing and mercury-using industries. Two years later, her *Industrial Poisons in the United States* was published, the first American text on the subject. Thanks to her efforts, in 1925, the surgeon general called a national conference on tetraethyl lead, then one on radium in 1928.

Always a student of foreign affairs, Hamilton served two terms (1924-30) as a member of the Health Committee of the League of Nations. Following its 1924 meeting in Geneva, she spent a month in the Soviet Union. Her reactions were mixed. She liked a land of "no rich people and few absolutely poverty-stricken." She found the nation advanced in industrial hygiene and its treatment of tuberculosis; she envied the women doctors there, for men and women in medicine were absolutely equal. On the other hand, she deplored the suppression of personal liberty, the concentration of power in a few, and the fanaticism of party members.

Hamilton was forced to retire from Harvard in 1935, when she was 66. She made her home in Hadlyme rather than Boston. For the next 14 years, she was still active professionally. Under Frances Perkins, then secretary of Labor, she became a medical consultant. In this capacity, from 1937 to 1938, she made her last detailed study of the poisonous trades. The culprit was carbon disulfide, used in the manufacture of viscose rayon. Its fumes could cause paralysis as well as serious psychiatric reactions, but the danger of this compound was almost unknown in the United States. After publication of her medical findings in Pennsylvania, a state law was passed there to grant occupational disease compensation to victims. In addition, radical reform was made in working conditions in that state's viscose rayon plants.

The study was soon extended to other states. The results were gratifying. Hamilton noted that the changes came with rapidity: Engineers developed methods to prevent the escape of fumes; regular examination of the workers ensured that early signs of toxicity would be recognized; and routine analyses of the air provided detection of excessive amounts of carbon disulfide or hydrogen sulfide. Alice had been, as so often before, the prime mover in pointing out the danger. But she did not stop there; she suggested improvements and lobbied for legislation.

A meeting of the International Congress of Occupational Accidents and

Diseases brought her to Germany in 1938. (She had had exposure to Nazism in 1933.) Missing in 1938 were Jews, Russians and Czechs. She wrote about hearing Hitler speak on the radio. From that 100-minute tirade against the Czechs, "there was not one noble, lofty idea, only hate, hate and lies, which he knew were lies. Yet the Germans worshiped him."

Alice Hamilton's autobiography, *Exploring the Dangerous Trades*, came out in 1943. The illustrations were done by Norah Hamilton. Six years later, a revision of Hamilton's 1934 textbook on industrial technology was published with co-author Harriet Hardy, an authority on beryllium toxicity.

Hamilton remained physically active in her 80s, although deafness was becoming increasingly bothersome. At 88 she was able to say, "I wouldn't change my life a bit." Many honors came her way. As a tribute to her ninetieth birthday, those who were associated with her professionally set up the Alice Hamilton Fund for Occupational Medicine at the Harvard School of Public Health. President Nixon sent her a congratulatory note on her one hundredth birthday. (Her activities were very restricted in her 90s.) In 1970 she died of a stroke at the age of 101. In 1995 a 55-cent postage stamp was issued in her honor.

Alice Hamilton was a trained scientist. Her unique contributions to society had roots in her long association with Hull House. Living among poor immigrants gave her remarkable insight into their problems. She realized that any wage earner has a fear of sickness, of unemployment and of old age, and the endless stream of liberal thinkers who came and went stimulated her thinking in this area.

Alice's letters and writing give glimpses of this thinking, which was independent and not always completely associated with a group or movement. She worked for contraception for poor women whose health and family would suffer from numerous births; at the same time, she did not approve of imposing family limitations on the poor, as did some in the eugenics movement. She was a strong pacifist with regard to World War I and Vietnam; she changed her thinking during World War II. Originally opposed to the Equal Rights Amendment (ERA) in 1921 because she thought it would harm protective legislation for women, she reversed her stand in 1952. Possessed of a strong Protestant religious faith, her friends included Jews, nonbelievers and so on — she respected an individual's integrity and was not concerned with his religious beliefs. She favored socialism, but maintained very good personal relations with men who headed successful capitalistic enterprises.

Hamilton saw the difficulties encountered by women doctors but stated: "I have never suffered from them myself. During the period of my laboratory work I could join any scientific society and speak and publish as freely as if I were a man. And when I went into industrial medicine I often felt that my sex was a help, not a handicap. Employees and doctors both appeared more willing to listen to me as I told them their duty toward their employees and patients than they would have if I had been a man."

# Chapter 6

# Florence Sabin
*Histologist and Public Servant*

*Excellence is never granted to man, but as the reward of labour.* — Sir Joshua Reynolds

Florence Rena Sabin, M.D., had an unusual career; she first distinguished herself in research and teaching. After retirement from a research position, she worked assiduously for reform of public health in the state of Colorado.

She was born on November 9, 1871, in Central City, Colorado, to George K. Sabin and Serena (Miner) Sabin. The second of two girls, she lost two younger brothers who died in infancy. Her parents were transplanted New Englanders: George had come west in 1860 to make money in mining; Serena arrived seven years later to teach.

When Florence was 7, her mother died as a result of childbirth. Mary, the older child, and Florence spent a short period in boarding school, then lived for four happy years in Chicago with the family of an uncle, Albert Sabin. Through his influence, she developed a sense of security, an appreciation of music, a love of nature, an interest in reading and, best of all, a capacity for sympathy and understanding of others.

When she was 12, Florence moved to Vermont to be near her paternal grandparents in Rockingham. For five years she studied at a private school, Vermont Academy in Saxtons River. Making her mark there as a good student and gifted pianist, she graduated in 1889.

Mary Sabin was enrolled at Smith College in Northampton, Massachusetts, when Florence entered as a freshman. The sisters lived together in a private house. Apparently they had no financial problems. Florence enjoyed the curriculum and did well. A zoology course in her junior year convinced her that she had to become a doctor. (Her father had wanted to study medicine, but got involved in mining.) Florence accepted the fact that she lacked

**Florence Sabin**
**(Courtesy National Library of Medicine)**

good looks and had to wear glasses; this may have contributed to her decision to reject marriage in favor of a demanding career.

To earn money for medical school, Florence taught mathematics for the next two years at Wolfe Hall, the Denver school in which she and Mary had been placed as children; a third year was spent at her alma mater in Northampton. During this period, she became acquainted with the family of Ella Strong Denison, a woman whose friendship she enjoyed until Mrs. Denison's death in 1940.

Sabin entered the medical school of Johns Hopkins University in 1896, when she was 25. A member of the fourth class of this new medical school, she had no difficulty in being admitted, despite her sex and the high standards. Women controlled resources that had made the school possible, and these women had stipulated that females be admitted under the same terms as men, and that high admittance standards be imposed. Thus Florence was able to obtain a first class medical education, for Hopkins proved to be an outstanding school.

She was especially enthusiastic about the teaching of Franklin P. Mall, professor of anatomy, and he seemed to recognize her potential. While still a second-year student, she had a neuroanatomy article published in the *Johns Hopkins Hospital Bulletin*. Under Mall's guidance, she constructed a three-dimensional model of part of the brain and wrote an accompanying laboratory manual entitled *An Atlas of the Medulla and Mid-brain*. (Published in 1901, this became a popular text.) Her fellow classmates appear to have respected her; one noted that she was the first woman he had ever met who showed no prudery in sex anatomy and physiology. During her medical school years, Sabin showed an interest in social issues — for example, she helped to produce the Maryland *Suffrage News*, a weekly paper. She also developed a lifelong friendship with Mabel Glover Mall, the wife of her mentor.

After graduation in 1900, Sabin did an internship in internal medicine under Osler — a great honor. But she became aware that the practice of medicine had less appeal for her than did the laboratory. Mall encouraged her to become a research scientist, and she took his advice.

Her salary for the first year in the department of anatomy was paid for by a fellowship donated by the Baltimore Women's Committee. (Organized by M. Carey Thomas, later president of Bryn Mawr College, it was this committee and Dr. Thomas who played a significant role in securing the admission of women to the medical school of Johns Hopkins University.) In 1902 she was hired by the university, winning its first medical school appointment given a woman. She remained at Hopkins until 1925, active in research and teaching. Sabin was not a militant feminist, but believed strongly in equality of opportunity for women. She must have felt some responsibility in setting an example for other women to follow

Sabin began in 1900 a continuing investigation of the lymphatic system, then poorly understood. She studied the origin of lymphatic vessels, then turned her attention to the origin of blood vessels and the development of blood cells, especially those involved in immune reactions. By injecting dye into small pig embryos, she showed that the lymphatics arose directly from veins. This work was impressive enough to prompt an invitation for her to write a chapter in the *Manual of Human Embryology* (1910-12). Summer visits to German laboratories stimulated her interest in new approaches and techniques in microscopy — for example, the use of dyes to observe live cells, rather than fixed preparations. She studied living chick embryos in hanging drop preparations. She described the excitement of watching blood vessels form, of seeing the precursors of the red and white blood cells, of watching the heart's first beat take place. Her investigation of the blood cells focused on the monocytes — cells that are characteristic of tubercles, the lesions of tuberculosis.

An appointment in the anatomy department meant teaching duties. Sabin was an excellent instructor — she became better known for her teaching than her research. With Mall, she believed that a great educator must himself be an investigator. She was enthusiastic about her subject — histology — which covers the microscopic appearance of tissues. At first she was an assistant to Ross Harrison, the eminent zoologist; after 1907, she was in charge. In 1911, William Welch, then dean, noted that "one of the most successful teachers on our faculty is a woman." She held firmly that it was more important for the student to be able to find out something for himself rather than memorize statements made by someone else. In 1917 she was promoted to the rank of professor. However, after Mall's death, she had been passed over for the chairmanship of the department, despite the circulation of a student petition on her behalf and despite protest from the Baltimore Women's Committee. Ironically, the candidate chosen was one of her students.

McMaster and Heidelberger pointed out that Sabin's influence on the improvement of the lot of women was immense; she accomplished much more by the example of her work than she could have as a mere advocate of reform. Her scientific reputation was becoming known to the public: When Madame Curie visited the United States in 1921, Sabin was selected to greet that great physicist on behalf of the women scientists of the United States.

In 1925, Sabin, then 54, became a research scientist at the Rockefeller Institute for Medical Research (now Rockefeller University). At the request of Simon Flexner, its director, she set up a section on cellular immunity. The subject under investigation was tuberculosis, still a serious menace to health. For 13 years, Florence and her coworkers studied the immune aspects of tuberculosis.

During her tenure at Rockefeller, she wrote *Franklin Paine Mall: The Story of a Mind.* The project took about five years, but Sabin wanted to do justice to the man who had inspired her. When the biography was published in 1934, it was well received.

Florence retired in 1938 to live in Colorado with Mary. After some years of relative inactivity, she began, at 73, a new career. Appointed by Governor John Vivian to a planning committee on postwar public health problems, she was considered by some a nice old lady who knew little about medicine other than from the laboratory standpoint, and one who would make no waves.

These people found that the nice old lady let the public know that the board of health was inefficient, under political control and operating with inadequate funding. The committee she headed drafted a legislative program ("Sabin program") of six bills. These measures: (1) provided for a complete reorganization of the state's health department; (2) allowed adjoining counties with limited resources to receive federal, state or local funds to organize district health services; (3) set up a state tuberculosis hospital; (4) increased the per diem allowance for hospitalized indigent tuberculous patients; (5) established strict control of brucellosis, rampant in Colorado cattle; and (6) gave authority to the state department of public health to receive federal funds for hospital construction. Sabin did not support the third measure but worked indefatigably for the others. She visited each of the state's 63 counties to campaign. She was received with enthusiasm and respect and had very favorable coverage by newspapers. By 1947, six of the eight reforms she proposed had passed the legislature, thanks largely to her personal lobbying efforts.

She next served as manager of health and charity for Denver. (Denver operated under a "home-rule principle" that made it exempt from the new state health regulations.) Continuing the reforms now required by the state, Sabin improved restaurant sanitation. She also, in two years, cut in half the city's death rate from tuberculosis by providing free X-rays. She donated her salary to the support of medical research at the University of Colorado. When she resigned, it was to care for her ailing sister.

Florence died in Denver on October 3, 1954, while watching a baseball game on television. She was 81.

Florence Sabin's bookplate had a quote: "Thou, O God, dost sell unto us all good things at the price of labour." Her price of labor was exemplified by her total involvement in the problem at hand. Although she had broad interests — among them reading, Oriental art, music, cooking, the Brooklyn Dodgers — she submerged herself in her work, which she carried on with efficiency and enthusiasm.

When she was young, she encouraged married women to have careers. An older Florence had some doubts about this. Perhaps she realized that a woman with a husband and children might not be free to devote as much time to her profession as she did. When once asked by the daughter of a friend about entering medical school, her reply was that she did not think good-looking girls such as the inquirer should become doctors because they will work for a few years and then get married.

On the occasion of Florence's eightieth birthday, a colleague named Henry Swan wrote a tribute that very well expressed her life's work:

> To have meant so much to so many people, to have influenced their lives to be more productive and more satisfying, and in the meanwhile to have added so much to the storehouse of scientific understanding, is to have built the most beautiful and enduring personal monument within the scope of human capacity.

For her achievements she received many honors. She was elected in 1925 to the National Academy of Sciences, a body that extends membership only to those who have made significant scientific contributions. She was the first woman so honored in the 86 years of the academy's existence. Her native state paid her homage by placing her likeness in bronze, sculpted by Joy Buba, in Statuary Hall of the nation's capitol. These honors represent Florence Sabin, distinguished scientist, and Florence Sabin, determined advocate of health reform. In each role, she represented high competence.

# Chapter 7

# Josephine Baker
## Pioneer Physician in Child Care

*A wise man should consider that health is the greatest of human blessings.* — Hippocrates

As did Alice Hamilton, Josephine Baker used her scientific training to bring about innovative improvements in existing social conditions.

She was born on November 15, 1873, and named Sara Josephine Baker. However, it was only late in life that she used the first name to avoid confusion with the famous dancer. Her birthplace was Poughkeepsie, New York, and her parents were Orlando Daniel Mosher Baker and Jennie (Harwood) Baker; there were two other girls and a boy, each of whom died before reaching adulthood. The parents had roots in the United States; the father was a successful lawyer, the mother an early graduate of Vassar College.

With the expectation that she would attend Vassar, Josephine was educated in a good private school. Her instruction in practical matters was not overlooked: A dressmaker came to the Baker home twice a year for a six-week period to make summer or winter outfits for the female members of the family, at the same time teaching Josephine the art of seamstressing. Learning to cook was another part of Josephine's education. Her youth was carefree. She remembered bobsledding as well as ice skating and ice boating on the Hudson. At a young age she fished with her father, trying to make it up to him for being a girl. When she was older, she played tennis, attended formal luncheons and gay balls as well as concerts and other such events.

This comfortable existence ended with the death of O.D.M. Baker from typhoid fever when Josephine was 16. It was clear that someone would have to support the family, then consisting of her mother, Josephine and a sister named Mary, who was a semi-invalid. The decision was made that Josephine study medicine; with a medical degree she would be able to pay the family's bills. It was agreed that she should have $5,000 from her father's small estate to pay for her professional education.

Her plan to obtain a degree from Vassar had to be abandoned. After a year's study at home, she received certification by the New York State Board of Regents that allowed her to enroll at the medical college for women then affiliated with the New York Infirmary for Women and Children. (The medical school no longer exists.)

The four-year course offered good training, and she graduated in 1898, second in a class of 18. One of her classmates was Florence Laighton, with whom she would live and practice for many years. Ironically, the child-care authority to-be failed a sophomore course entitled "The Normal Child." It had bored her, but repeating it whetted her interest and had a direct influence on her career in preventive medicine.

An internship at the New England Hospital for Women and Children followed graduation. In her entertaining autobiography, Baker described the patients:

> We were dealing with the dregs of Boston, ignorant, shiftless, settled irrevocably into surly degradation. Just to be sure they would be hopeless, many of them drank savagely. Having borne children and lived and fought and made love regardless, they took that method of dodging the consequences. Nothing admirable about it, but one could not honestly blame them for making use of alcohol as an anesthetic.

With help from Florence Laighton's family, Josephine and Florence set up in New York City a private practice that continued until 1914. They even invested in a car, a Prescott steamer, the water supply for which lasted only 20 miles.

The medical practice was not successful at first, and to earn extra cash, in 1901, Baker took an additional position in the city's Department of Health, a department associated with a corrupt political system. (Ironically, she got the job through pull, chiefly because her father was known. She placed eighth of the 800 who took the required civil service examination; the rule was that the position go to one of the top three.)

One of her jobs was to make a medical inspection of school children. However, so little time was allotted for such investigations, the effort seemed to the young doctor "a pathetic farce."

The situation improved when a new mayor and health commissioner came on the scene. The causative agents of many contagious diseases were then known, and the germ theory of disease was taken seriously. Public health was a field where new knowledge could be used effectively in the right hands.

A summer position with the department at $100 a month gave Baker experience in the old "Hell's Kitchen" area of New York's East Side. She was to find and care for sick babies. According to her: "I climbed stair after stair,

**Josephine Baker**
(Courtesy New York City Health and Hospitals Corporation. Redrawn by Mary Frey.)

knocked on door after door, met drunk after drunk, filthy mother after mother and dying baby after dying baby.... It depressed me so that I branched out and went looking for healthy babies too and tried to tell their mothers how to care for them. But they were not interested. I might as well have been trying to tell them how to keep it from raining." We have here a hint of her destiny.

In the course of her duties, Baker vaccinated people against smallpox. Sometimes this involved visits to Bowery lodging houses between midnight and 6 A.M., the hours when the lodgers were likely to be present. She investigated smoke hazards, plumbing and the like in overcrowded tenements where unspeakable conditions existed. An epidemic of cerebrospinal meningitis once occupied most of her energy for a short period. She wrote that her garb while on duty was devoid of feminine furbelows — she wore man-tailored suits.

By 1907, Baker had been appointed assistant to the health commissioner. It was in this capacity that she was sent to restrict the activities of Mary Mallon, better known as Typhoid Mary. This woman was a known carrier of typhoid fever, and it was necessary to prevent her from handling food.

The following year Baker became chief of the newly created Division of Child Hygiene — the first in the world. The success of this division made its founding in 1908 a significant date in public health history.

Baker had an idea, and 30 nurses were assigned to her to execute it: She would attack the high infant mortality rate that New York experienced in summer. Some 1,500 babies died, mainly from diarrhea, each week of the hot summer months. The name and address of every newborn baby in a specific area were obtained from the registrar of records the day after the infant's birth. A public health nurse immediately made a visit to the mother — usually an immigrant with little or no knowledge of the essentials of health care. These nurses emphasized basic procedures such as breast feeding (to avoid contaminated milk), frequent bathing, efficient ventilation and suitable clothing for summer.

After about two months, the records showed that there were 1,200 fewer deaths in the designated district than there had been during the same period of the previous year. The success was due to simple preventive medicine, but at the time it represented new thinking. Having no precepts to follow, Baker proceeded as she saw fit, based on her training, observations, and deductions.

She confronted the problem of midwives. Italian, Hungarian, Polish, Armenian, Greek and Slovak women immigrants were accustomed to midwives; most could not afford female physicians, and few immigrants, whether or not they had the money, would allow themselves to be delivered by male physicians. In New York, the typical midwife left much to be desired, mainly because of her ignorance. Under Baker's leadership, new and stringent licensing laws were drawn up with the purpose of locating all of the practicing midwives in the city, providing an opportunity to deal with the unfit. By 1911 a special school of obstetrics had been started at Bellevue Hospital. From then on, licenses were granted only to graduates of this school or of European schools of similar quality.

Once there were qualified midwives, the bureau required that they use a drop of silver nitrate in each eye of the newborn immediately after birth to prevent gonorrheal infection, which could cause blindness. (Gonorrhea was not uncommon in mothers and could infect the infant during the birth process.) The bureau was behind designing packaging for the silver nitrate that ensured it remained at the correct concentration.

Baker even designed baby clothes that made it easier to dress squirming infants. The McCall Pattern Company bought the idea and sold sets of patterns for it, paying her a royalty of one cent each. The Metropolitan Life Insurance Company ordered 200,000 for their policyholders.

Baker was concerned with the high death rate in one large foundling hospital where good medical care existed. Although the idea of maternal deprivation was unknown at the time, she effectively halved the mortality rate by supplying loving foster parents to care for the babies in their own houses in the slums. The Russell Sage Foundation aided in this endeavor. (This writer is not convinced that the establishment of a child-maternal relationship was the sole cause of the improvement in child mortality.)

As a way to teach proper child care to ignorant mothers, in 1916, the bureau set up "Baby Health Stations," at first aided by funds raised privately by Mrs. J. Borden Harriman. The stations sold bottled pasteurized milk for a few cents less than the price of grocery store milk. The latter was not regulated by law, was unpasteurized because of prejudice against "cooked" milk, and was likely to cause disease. The cheaper milk sold well, and the mothers who came to get it were taught fundamentals of child care. "Everything you taught," wrote Baker, "had to be simple and standardized enough to fit [the mother's] mentality." The project was so successful that it was eventually financed by public funds. By the time Josephine left office, it involved 60,000 babies a year.

In 1910, Baker read in John Spargo's *The Bitter Cry of the Children* about the "little mother"— a girl in a poor family who had to take care of the next-youngest child because the mother was forced to work. Josephine was familiar with New York's slum little mother —"a scrawny child of 8 or 9, dirty and dishevelled, lugging a dirtier and more dishevelled baby." Spargo believed that there should be no such thing as a little mother who innocently caused the annual death of thousands of children.

Baker knew that in countless tenement families that little mother was a necessity. Being of a practical nature, she organized Little Mothers Leagues in the schools. Here nurses taught young girls the essentials of baby care. Then the girls themselves served as missionaries, spreading their new knowledge to the slums. The idea caught on, not only in the United States, but overseas, and the leagues were in operation for many years.

The Bureau of Child Hygiene was at first involved with common contagious diseases such as measles, scarlet fever, chickenpox, mumps and whooping cough. Later there was emphasis on dental care, good vision, classroom ventilation and the like. By 1915 the work had become so demanding that Josephine was forced to give up her by-then very successful private practice to work full time for the city.

Beginning in 1916, she lectured on child hygiene every year for the next 15 years at New York University–Bellevue Hospital Medical School. In 1917 she received the degree of Doctor of Public health from New York University, becoming the first woman recipient. Her thesis was about the relationship between classroom ventilation and respiratory diseases among school children. Her figures showed the value of open window ventilation, a practice not then followed.

An epidemic of poliomyelitis in 1916 caused a degree of panic never equalled in the history of the New York Health department. (Vaccines against the disease were not generally available until the 1950s, and the thought of paralysis was terrifying to every family.)

When food was scarce during World War I, the bureau used various means to combat malnutrition in children. It was during this time that Baker made a statement that drew attention to her cause: "It's six times safer to be a soldier in the trenches of France than to be born a baby in the United States." That statement and the plight of refugee European children prompted other states to establish bureaus similar to Josephine's. The concepts she advocated were also well received by other countries, and representatives from France, Germany, Russia, England, China, and Japan flocked to New York to learn how to organize effective child hygiene units. Josephine enjoyed the personal contacts that this entailed.

Baker was a pioneer in her field. Men were not used to a woman in a municipal executive position. A pragmatist, she seemed to make progress by dealing successfully with people and situations on an individual basis. Also, in the course of her work, she came into contact with the great and near-great of her day — for example, Theodore Roosevelt, Woodrow Wilson, Fannie Hurst and Amy Lowell. She interacted with them as well as she did with her mothers and coworkers. She was practical enough to accept from time to time existing conditions of which she disapproved, using them as a starting point to make needed improvements.

Her sense of humor must have been an asset — her autobiography shows a real wit. For instance, she recounted that at one of the many luncheons where she was a guest speaker, an august chairman whispered deferentially, "Will you speak now, Dr. Baker, or shall I let them enjoy themselves a little longer?" Another example is her description of a method that pediatricians used to modify cow's milk for young babies — a method too complicated for tenement mothers to use. The method was, she wrote, "based on consideration of the baby's age, health, complexion, nationality, color of eyes and numerological and astrological data — at least so it seemed when you started working with it." (Her response to the problem was to base the addition of water, lime water and milk sugar on the baby's weight.)

Baker had promised herself that when the forty-eighth state had organized a bureau of child hygiene, she would retire. That came about in 1923, and she resigned. By then, New York City's infant mortality rate had dropped from 111 to 66 per 1,000 live births — the lowest to that time found in major cities in Europe and America

Josephine remained active after her retirement. From 1924 to 1925 she was a member of the Health Committee of the League of Nations. She worked for various causes important to her, among them women's suffrage and the prevention of child labor. The first she considered a matter of simple justice. She was bitterly disappointed in the negligible consequences of giving women the vote; in 1939 she wrote that one example of how American women failed to keep the promise of bonding together to improve social and political conditions — part of suffragist propaganda — was that the child labor amendment was still unratified.

She spent three months in Russia with a friend who was gathering material for a book. Although Baker was not impressed with many aspects of that country, she left with a friendly attitude — unusual for an American in the 1930s.

Her final years were passed at her 200-year-old farm in Belle Mead, New Jersey. During her lifetime she wrote many professional and popular articles. She was also the author of four books, including the autobiographical *Fighting for Life*, published in 1939. She died of cancer in 1945 at the age of 75.

Although Josephine Baker had no children of her own, her work with children was rewarding as well as significant. She had reason to be proud of the information printed in a booklet published in 1939 by the Society of New York Hospital: "A child born this year will probably live fourteen years longer than one born twenty-five years ago. Expectancy of life has been increased through the prevention of disease and death during the first two years of life. There has been no greater gift than this in all the history of mankind."

# Chapter 8

# Mary Swartz Rose
## *Nutrition Educator*

*The period from 1890 to 1950 saw the establishment of a
definitive, medically sound nutrition.* — Roderick E.
McGrew

Mary Rose was a pioneer in the science of nutrition; she directed her
energy to making available to homemakers scientific knowledge about foods.
Unlike the women who are the subjects of the previous chapters of this book,
she was happily married and a mother.

She was born on October 31, 1874. Both parents were Ohio natives;
Hiram Swartz, a lawyer and judge, was of Dutch, German and Scottish
descent. Mary Jane (Davies) had Welsh forebears and was an educated woman.
The Swartzes belonged to the Protestant faith. Mary was born in Newark,
Ohio, the first of five children. When she was a young child, the family moved
to Wooster, where Mary attended local schools, graduating from high school
in 1892 as valedictorian of her class. Her father taught her Greek and Latin;
she learned shorthand and typing; she also played the guitar and sang. As an
adult, she went to current art exhibits, read Henry and William James, Henry
Adams, Ibsen, Willa Cather, A.A. Milne and Lewis Carroll; she was a scholar
of the Bible and had an interest in Chinese literature.

It would be some years before she obtained a bachelor's degree. In 1893
she entered the preparatory department of Shepardson College, where her mother
had studied. (Shepardson College was affiliated with Denison University, located
in Granville, Ohio.) Beginning the college course the following year, she
interrupted her plans in 1897 to teach at Wooster High School and study for
one year at the College of Wooster. Then she returned to Shepardson to complete the classical course in 1901. She has been described as being of small stature
and having an attractive and feminine appearance, a pleasing personality and
a cheerful disposition; she was also considered energetic and enthusiastic.

After graduation Swartz took a one-year diploma course in home economics at Mechanics Institute in Rochester, New York. For the next three years she taught home economics at the high school in Fond du Lac, Wisconsin. In 1905, she enrolled at Teachers College, Columbia University, obtaining a bachelor of science degree in household arts the next year. Her special interest was in the chemistry of food and nutrition. She remained at Teachers College for one year as an assistant and was then granted a teaching fellowship to study under the eminent Lafayette Mendel at Yale University. She obtained her Ph.D. degree in physiological chemistry in 1909.

After Yale, Swartz returned to Teachers College. An instructor in the new School of Household Arts, her charge was to establish a department of nutrition.

Some dietary-deficiency diseases, such as pellagra, were known, and research along these lines was being done. Knowledge in this field was being uncovered at a rapid rate, and Swartz participated in research as well as making the new knowledge understandable to students in the field and to the laity.

She was fortunate to have the collaboration of Henry Sherman, an expert in nutrition research and professor of food chemistry at Columbia. Her own department became known nationally and internationally as a center where students received a scientific grounding in nutrition as well as excellent instruction in how to teach the subject. Over the years, approximately 11,000 students were enrolled in her various classes.

In 1910, the year when Mary became assistant professor, and when she was 35, she married Anton Richard Rose. Three years her junior, he had met her when he was studying physiological chemistry at Yale. It was apparently a happy marriage. Their only child was born in 1915, when Mary was 41. The family at first lived in Manhattan in an apartment. They later moved to Edgewater, New Jersey, where their home overlooking the Hudson became known for its beautiful grounds and gracious hostess. (The latter commuted to work by ferryboat, once announcing that she spent more time on the Edgewater Ferry than Noah had spent on the Ark.) From 1924 until 1948, Anton Rose worked for the Prudential Insurance Company, ultimately as director of its longevity laboratories. The three members of the Rose family were able to spend several summers traveling in Europe. According to Richard Rose, his father subordinated his career to his wife's, being supportive in every way. His mother was equally devoted to her husband, especially considering his needs and limitations as a diabetic.

Mary's professional activities were recognized; by 1921, she had attained the rank of professor. Her research emphasized practical application — for example, iron requirement in early childhood. Her *Laboratory Handbook for Dietetics* , written for students majoring in nutrition, went through four editions. The result of meticulous laboratory weighing of foods in many forms by Rose and students under her, it presented tables giving food values for

**Mary Swartz Rose**
**(Courtesy Columbia University Libraries)**

100-calorie portions, for one gram and for one ounce. Of this book, Grace MacLeod wrote, "Only those of us who were her students [before its publication] can fully appreciate what this meant in the saving of time and work in the laboratory." In 1916 she published *Everyday Foods in War Time*. The next year saw the first edition of her *Feeding the Family*. The wide acceptance of the latter by mothers and other homemakers was especially gratifying to Rose. *Foundations of Nutrition* (for non-nutrition majors) first appeared in 1928. The third edition, published in 1938, noted, "This book is written for those who wish to live more intelligently." Mary earned a reputation for presenting practical information about nutrition in clear, concise language.

A member of several professional associations, Rose was appointed in 1935 by the Health Committee of the League of Nations to study the physiological bases of nutrition. The assignment necessitated travel to Geneva and London.

Late in her career, she became involved in developing nutrition programs in the public schools. Her belief was that education in good eating habits ranked in importance with the subjects ordinarily taught, and she recognized that it is more difficult to change behavior after habits are formed than before they become established. With the aid of research grants, she made studies in ways to teach nutrition at various levels. In 1932 she wrote *Teaching Nutrition to Boys and Girls*, a book aimed at elementary school teachers. Note that she differentiated between nutrition and dietetics: "Nutrition deals with the scientific laws governing the requirements of human beings for maintenance, growth, activity, reproduction and lactation; dietetics with their practical application to individuals or groups in health and also in sickness."

Mary Rose retired in 1940. She died of cancer the following year, and was buried in Granville, Ohio. She lived to see Richard Rose finish at Middlebury College and complete graduate work in forestry at Yale.

Mary Rose approached the modern feminist goal — combining a successful career with marriage and motherhood. According to MacLeod: She could turn from exacting scientific research to preparations for a party in her home, the games and refreshments for which were the products of her own ingenuity and her deftness in cookery, or to plans for improvements in her house and garden, or to teaching her dog some new tricks, or to making a dress or a hat, or going to the theater or a movie for recreation with husband and son — all with a zest and vigor." Many who knew her considered her an expert in time management.

Margaret Rossiter, an authority on women scientists, has termed the science of nutrition "highly feminized." For this reason, some might consider a career in nutrition less desirable than other scientific careers. Nevertheless, Mary Rose's efforts advanced the status of nutrition, which remains an important branch of science.

In 1948, the Mary Swartz Rose Fellowship for graduate study in nutrition or allied fields was established by the Nutrition Foundation, Inc., and was awarded annually by the American Dietetic Association.

# Chapter 9

# Karen Horney
## *Psychiatrist*

*Self-reliance is [conformity's] aversion.*
— Ralph Waldo Emerson

When her investigations produced interpretations that disagreed with those of Sigmund Freud, Karen Horney did not shrink from publicizing her differences with the founder of psychoanalysis; she even refuted most of the fundamentals of his field. But, as a result, she developed a psychology of women.

Karen Clementine Theodora Danielsen was born near Hamburg, Germany, on September 15, 1885, to Berndt Henrik Wackels Danielsen and Clothilde Marie (Van Ronzelen) Danielsen. She was their only daughter and second child. Her father was of Norwegian origin, her mother from a Dutch-German family. The former, called Wackels, was a sea captain and often away on voyages to South and Central America for as long as six months. His wife, generally known as Sonni, was 17 years younger, beautiful, sophisticated and more liberal than her deeply religious and authoritarian husband. From him she inherited four teenage children, and there was rivalry between Sonni's children and her step-children. According to Karen's diaries, written in adolescence, the marriage was an unhappy one. Karen favored her mother over her father, but sometimes her feelings for Sonni were ambivalent.

When she was about 13, Karen attended a private school where she had exposure to a solid education. Her diary, which was begun around this time, is evidence that she was a perceptive, exceptionally bright student. By the time of her confirmation in the Lutheran church, she was beginning to question some of the tenets of the Bible.

In 1900, gymnasium classes were offered to girls for the first time in Hamburg. The German gymnasium was a secondary school designed to

**Karen Horney**
**(Courtesy Karen Horney Papers, Manuscripts and Archives, Yale University Library)**

prepare students for the university. The rigorous curriculum stressed the classics, history, mathematics and modern languages. Karen was enthusiastic about attending. Since it was novel for girls to be admitted to such a program, there was some doubt about whether Wackels would permit his daughter to go. Sonni was in favor of it, and in the end, the captain agreed.

As a gymnasium student, Danielsen had more independence than she had ever known. To get to school, she took a 32-minute train ride into the great port city of Hamburg; sometimes there was opportunity to visit the museum and to attend concerts and plays (which may have led to her brief aspirations to become an actress). Academically, she studied hard and did well.

It was during Karen's gymnasium days that Wackels and Sonni parted, later divorcing. Karen stayed with her mother, who tried to make ends meet by taking in boarders.

After the gymnasium, Danielsen passed the examination that admitted her to medical school. (After being permitted a gymnasium education, girls pressed successfully for entrance to the universities. Karen was one of 34 women entering the medical school at Freiburg.) Her diary writing showed that she was interested in certain young men, but apparently not interested enough to let marriage interfere with a career.

Sonni's separation meant that she and her family received less support from Wackels. Because of this, she soon moved — with some of her boarders — to Freiburg, where she would live with Karen. At times, Karen resented her mother's dependency on her.

Karen found medical school not only reasonably easy, but also to her liking. She even had time for a social life. Photographs show a somewhat plain young woman, but she seemed to be popular. In Freiburg she met Oskar Horney, who soon left to pursue a Ph.D. in political science, but later became her husband.

The two corresponded frequently. After she had finished two preclinical years in Freiburg and passed the state's written examinations in 1908, Karen went for clinical work to the University of Göttingen, in central Germany. Since Oskar was in nearby Braunschweig, their friendship grew. Oskar was not intimidated by Karen's ambition and independence. He, too, was ambitious, and soon found a promising position with a good industrial firm in Berlin. They were married there in 1909.

Horney continued her medical studies at the University of Berlin, receiving her master's degree in 1913. In 1910 she was psychoanalyzed by Karl Abraham. This brief experience whetted her interest in the new method and probably influenced her desire to practice psychiatry. (She later underwent additional psychoanalysis.)

A neurobiologist, Freud did not agree with German psychiatry, which regarded all mental aberrations as due entirely to organic changes. Early in his career, he was convinced that hysteria was due to emotional disturbance, not organic disease of the nervous system. His *Interpretation of Dreams* appeared in 1899. By 1908, 42 psychiatrists and psychologists attended the first international congress in psychoanalysis. Obviously, Horney was becoming involved in a new, but fast-growing, field.

Freud saw the unconscious as an area of great psychic activity that influenced personality and behavior; he believed that the repression of sexual urges was of central importance. Accordingly he developed psychoanalysis as a system of interpretation and treatment of psychological disorders.

Horney's training in psychiatry emphasized diagnosis and was similar to that given in neurology, the branch of medicine dealing with the nervous system and its disorders. The German psychiatrists were inclined to look on psychoanalysis with contempt (it was, and is, beyond the scope of ordinary tests for scientific reliability). Nevertheless, Freudian psychoanalysis remained the most widely used method of psychotherapy until at least the 1950s.

In 1910, Horney suffered a period of depression. Her first child, Brigitte, was born in 1911, and, by 1915, Marianne and Renate had arrived. Between 1915 and 1918, Karen treated German soldiers suffering from what was known as shell shock during the Great War. In 1917 she read a paper to sexologists on the technique of psychoanalysis. She took her first psychoanalytic patients in 1919.

Oskar was making plenty of money. The family lived well, relatively isolated from the terrible events of the war, although Brigitte did contract tuberculosis, then rampant in Berlin. In 1918 they moved to a new Berlin suburb named Zehlendorf, where they lived in affluence and where Karen saw her private patients. These patients were middle-class women like herself. Brigitte and Marianne later remembered their mother at this time as deeply involved in her profession. She loved them, but left their care to others.

Karen's faith in psychoanalysis was so great that she arranged to have her three daughters begin psychoanalysis, although not one had displayed symptoms that ordinarily warrant such action. She admitted later that it was not a good idea.

The extraordinary inflation that occurred in Germany in 1923 had a marked effect on the Horneys. When Oskar's employer became a victim, Oskar lost his position. After that, he became involved in several unsuccessful ventures and was soon bankrupt. In 1926 the Horneys were forced to sell their luxurious home.

The Horney marriage did not survive the strain imposed by the financial situation and a serious illness that befell Oskar. They soon separated, although there was not a divorce until 1937. Both had been involved in extramarital affairs. Karen would have lovers for the rest of her life.

The six years following the separation from Oskar proved to be productive for Karen, then in her 40s. She was actively involved in the Berlin Psychoanalytic Clinic and Institute, first as lecturer, then as training and supervising analyst. Psychoanalysis is required of doctors and psychologists who intend to practice psychoanalysis, and throughout her career much of Horney's time and talent were spent in training prospective psychoanalysts. The Berlin Institute, which she helped to found, became a magnet for professionals from many countries. It provided free analytic treatment to many people, and, beginning in 1927, inpatient treatment for a limited number of severely disturbed patients. Horney's colleagues became her close friends. During this period she wrote a series of papers that addressed female psychology and sexuality. Her statements opposed Freud's ideas about female psychology, and to publicize any difference with such an authority took considerable confidence and courage.

She appears to have had adequate financial resources. At first, it was necessary to have a renter in the family apartment, but soon the Horney daughters appeared to be well provided for, and Karen herself seemed to lead a comfortable existence.

In 1932 Franz Alexander, a former member of the Berlin Institute, invited Karen to become his second-in-command at Chicago's Institute for Psychoanalysis, which he headed. With the Nazi rise to power in Germany, many Jewish psychiatrists were leaving that country. Horney was not Jewish, but what was happening in Germany was offensive to her liberal views. Deciding to take Alexander's offer, she sailed for New York with 15-year-old Renate. Brigitte, in training to become an actress, and Marianne, a medical student, continued their studies in Germany.

In Chicago, Karen was somewhat of a personage. Although the United States was in the depths of the Depression, expensive psychoanalysis was regarded as a beneficial European import. Nevertheless, she had to face a different way of life, to become more fluent in English and to take licensing examinations to practice medicine. It was a difficult adjustment, but Horney was flexible. Early in 1933, she filed a declaration of intention to become an American citizen. That fall, following a vacation in Switzerland with her three daughters, she returned to Chicago with Marianne, who planned to finish her medical studies at the University of Chicago.

By her second year in the United States, Horney had a German housekeeper, had bought some American stocks and was the possessor of a car, although, according to one daughter, her mother was anything but a good driver. During the Chicago years also, Karen's intellectual relationship with Erich Fromm, the psychoanalyst who was 15 years her junior, changed to a romantic one. One of the students whom she supervised at the time described her as lacking in sex appeal, decidedly a maternal type; of medium to largish build, she often displayed a manner of "great benignity." Others noted that she possessed unusual personal magnetism.

By 1934 Horney was in New York City to stay. There were several reasons for her leaving Chicago, the most important being conflict between her and Alexander, her chief. According to his official explanation, he had admired her independent thinking (in Berlin), but was unaware of the deeply rooted resentment she harbored against Freud; she, according to Alexander, was attempting to revise the whole psychoanalytic doctrine, but did not succeed in substituting anything substantially new and valid.

In New York, Horney associated herself with the New York Psychoanalytic Institute and the New School for Social Research. The latter was recruiting European psychoanalysts to its staff, and many émigrés joined. Karen supervised the training of psychoanalysts, gave lectures and published her ideas. As a lecturer, she drew large audiences.

Her first book, *The Neurotic Personality of Our Times*, was published in 1937 and was very well received. Others followed. They appealed to both laymen and professionals, and brought her income and, indirectly, new patients. She had a facility for putting complex ideas into simple language. Various readers noted that in the material they found self-recognition.

Among the refugee professionals — most of whom were intellectuals and some of whom had liberal political persuasions — Horney felt at home. She made many friends, such as theologian Paul Tillich and his wife. Fromm was also in New York. Soon she had money to spare, some of which she spent for a combined office and apartment. She also built a country home in Croton on the Hudson River. (She would be involved in real estate deals for the rest of her life.) She began to wear more elegant clothes than had been her custom. She obtained American citizenship in 1938, the year before the beginning of World War II.

Karen became a grandmother in 1936 when Renate had a daughter named Kaya, the nickname for Karen when she was a child. Renate, who had married her high school sweetheart, later moved to Mexico to escape the Nazi regime; Brigitte became a film star in Germany; after graduation from medical school, Marianne chose psychiatry as her specialty.

Exiled from Austria, Freud died in England in 1939, just a few months after the publication of Horney's second book, *New Ways in Psychoanalysis.* Its criticism of the old man, dying of cancer, angered some of his most loyal followers. Another reason for the growing censure of Horney might have been that, as a non–Jew, she had suffered little from the Nazis. On the other hand, Freud and many of his followers had been persecuted because they were Jewish, and some Jewish colleagues found Karen callous. She was extremely popular as a teacher, which may have provoked jealousy in some of her cohorts. Whatever the reasons, in 1941, the Educational Committee of the New York Psychoanalytic Society voted to demote Horney from instructor to lecturer. Karen resigned immediately. Others on the staff also resigned in protest.

The splinter faction very soon founded its own Association for the Advancement of Psychoanalysis with a publication named the *American Journal of Psychoanalysis.* Its teaching arm was the American Institute for Psychoanalysis, of which Horney was dean. Membership was somewhat depleted after the entrance of the United States into World War II, but steady progress was made. Members taught at the New School and at the Post-Graduate School of the New York Medical College at Flower Fifth Avenue Hospital. Horney's *Self-Analysis* was published early in 1942, adding to her recognition among lay people. The leading lights in the new organization were Horney, another psychiatrist named Clara Thompson and nonpsychiatrist Erich Fromm. Karen did not lack private patients; she had far too many referred to her to treat herself. On the negative side, the training program that she represented was recognized by neither the American Psychoanalytic Association nor the International Psychoanalytic Association, as was that of the New York Psychoanalytic Society.

Ironically, there was soon the all-too-familiar infighting in the new organization, followed by splits. One of the members who left was Fromm; Horney's relationship with him had ended, and this may have been a reason for his leaving.

Harold Kelman became president of the Association for the Advancement of Psychoanalysis. He lacked Horney's teaching ability, but was strong in organizational skills. He and Karen saw eye to eye about many matters, and she came to depend on him. He in turn "played vessel" to "Horney's queen," as one of the students put it. Affairs ran smoothly until 1948, when differences arose between Kelman and Frederick Weiss, a psychiatrist whom Horney began to support rather than Kelman.

As Horney grew older, she took longer vacations, often to Mexico to visit her family. She acquired a cocker spaniel. She also began a liaison with a younger man who was one of her patients. The affair lasted until she died.

Horney was still interested in treatment, but writing had become her chief concern. In 1945 *Our Inner Conflicts* came out, and, five years later, *Neurosis and Human Growth*.

Through Daisetz Suzuki, who was teaching at Columbia University, Horney became enthusiastic about Zen Buddhism. This was not surprising — she had long ago sought to understand religion. In 1952 she and Brigitte flew to Japan for a five-week visit. Their party was accompanied by Suzuki himself, who planned their visits to Zen temples. Karen considered the Japan stay one of the greatest experiences of her life.

Around two months after her return to New York, she became ill. The diagnosis was cancer with metastasis, and she died on December 4, 1952. Paul Tillich conducted the funeral service.

Today the Association for the Advancement of Psychoanalysis exists in New York City as the Karen Horney Psychoanalytic Institute. It is affiliated with the Karen Horney Clinic; both are fully accredited. However, psychoanalysis is only one among many types of psychotherapy used in psychiatry.

Horney's major contribution is her concept of female psychology, much of which is not in agreement with Freud because she attempted to form a theory that fitted her medical experience. From the beginning, she rejected Freudian phallocentric psychology, with its emphasis on castration, female inferiority and the importance of penis envy in the psychosexual development of women. She refused to accept feminine psychology as an offshoot of masculine psychology. Influenced by the writings of sociologist Georg Simmel and psychologist Georg Groddeck, she emphasized the influence of the male-dominated culture on female psychology — an influence that creates feelings of inferiority. She theorized that social and environmental factors, as opposed to the biological favored by Freud, play a major role in the causes of personality disorders.

According to psychiatrist Jack Rubin, most of Horney's ideas have quietly entered the mainstream of psychology. Her most recent biographer,

Bernard Paris, pointed out that Horneyan theory may be usefully employed in the study not only of gender, but of literature, biography and culture. Such studies have been published on Shakespeare, Emily Brönte, Dickens and Hemingway, among others. Horneyan analysis has been exemplified in psychobiographies of Robert Frost, Josef Stalin, Lyndon Johnson and others.

In 1967 Harold Kelman translated and compiled Horney's early works as *Female Psychology*. This aided feminists' recognition of her writings as allied to their thinking.

By 1996, Karen Horney was ranked thirty-fourth in Deborah Felder's *100 Most Important Women of All Time: A Ranking Past and Present.*

# Chapter 10

# Libbie Hyman
## *Zoologist*

...*in order categorical.* — Sir William Gilbert

This is the portrait of a scientist who preferred to write about the classification of animals rather than do experimental work. She followed her desire, gaining world renown.

Libbie Henrietta Hyman was born in Des Moines, Iowa, on December 6, 1888, the only daughter and the third of four children. Her parents were Jewish immigrants: Joseph Hyman was Polish; Sabina (Neumann) Hyman was German. Libbie grew up in Fort Dodge, Iowa, loving the woods and the wonders of nature. At home, however, her life was not happy. Her father, a tailor, was inept at business, with the result that the family was impoverished. Her mother, 20 years younger than Joseph, was domineering and selfish. Libbie herself apparently had few friends, and led a somewhat isolated life. The unfortunate home situation did not prevent her from graduating from high school in 1905, the valedictorian and youngest member of her class.

Eager to learn more, she returned to the high school for a fifth year to take science courses she had missed and also additional classes in German. She was still too young to teach, so she found a job at a local factory where she pasted labels on boxes of Mother's Rolled Oats. During this short stint, one of her former high school teachers was instrumental in getting Hyman a scholarship to the University of Chicago, which she entered in 1906. Eventually she earned there not only a bachelor's degree (with honors in zoology) but also a Ph.D. All her tuition was paid for by scholarships, the annual awarding of which was contingent on the previous year's work. To earn needed cash, there were oncampus jobs such as that of cashier at the Women's Commons.

After Joseph Hyman died in 1907, the family moved to Chicago. Libbie then lived at home with her mother and unmarried brothers until the former's death in 1940.

Although Libbie's original intention was to be a botanist, she was disappointed in what she considered anti–Semitism in the Department of Botany at the University of Chicago. After finding chemistry not exactly to her liking, she was influenced by a woman laboratory assistant in zoology who urged her to specialize in that field.

Consequently, during her senior year, Hyman took a course given by Charles Manning Field, an authority on invertebrates and famous for his research on metabolism. She found invertebrates so interesting that she took the Ph.D. under Field's direction and also remained in his laboratory until 1931. Many of Libbie's publications covered research projects connected with Field's work.

During her Chicago tenure, Hyman developed valuable assets. Besides becoming a real authority on invertebrates, particularly on flatworms, her scientific writing came to be regarded as accurate and exceptionally clear. At the suggestion of University of Chicago Press personnel, she wrote *Laboratory Manual for Elementary Zoology*, which was published in 1919. With vertebrate anatomy a required premedical course, her *Laboratory Manual of Comparative Vertebrate Anatomy*, published in 1922, was widely used. It was revised and expanded in 1942. In 1960, the author remarked that it had supported her in comfort if not in luxury for 30 years.

Hyman came to realize that a comprehensive reference work in English on the invertebrates was badly needed. She knew that she enjoyed study in taxonomy, or classification, and that she was gifted in presenting complex facts in writing. So it seemed logical to her to be the author of such a treatise. She had no illusions about the scope of the work — the invertebrates numbered around 1 million.

By 1931, with Sabina dead, Libbie was ready to start. The University of Chicago was willing to accommodate her, so that the work would be done there. But Hyman wanted to live elsewhere. At 43, she began the project by spending the first 15 months visiting scientists in Europe. Her itinerary included the Naples Zoological Station where Cornelia Clapp and Nettie Stevens had studied. She settled in New York City, finding a small apartment where she could live on the royalties from her books. New York City was attractive because it offered the library facilities required.

In preparing the first volume, which was not published until 1940, she ran into unanticipated difficulty. In her estimation, the work required illustrations, and she had assumed that the publisher would pay an artist to do them. The publisher would not, citing limited sales potential for the work she had undertaken. "You can do anything you have to," Hyman observed after she had produced numerous drawings herself— this despite the fact that she had always considered herself poor at drawing.

**Libbie Hyman**
**(Courtesy Department of Library Services,**
**American Museum of Natural History)**

By 1937 the American Museum of Natural History had given her a title without salary, plus office and laboratory space. She continued to work there until she died. In time she moved to a five-room house within commuting distance of the museum, living there for 11 years The property provided grounds where flowers would grow — and Libbie was known to prefer flower gardens even to laboratories. Still somewhat the same loner she had been in her youth, she had numerous acquaintances and correspondents from all over the world, most of them scientists. She was known for her candor, even in professional writing. Here is an example of the latter: "A fantastic theory that is to be utterly rejected...; there are no real grounds for this view, only theoretical vaporizings." Considering herself a scientist and her sex irrelevant, she once wrote a colleague that his organizing an all-women symposium was "a damned fool idea." She also decried the commercial importance placed on higher degrees. For a time she took on the editorship of *Systematic Zoology*. She suffered from Parkinson's disease during the last ten years of her life, spending the last two in a wheelchair.

*The Invertebrates*, which ran to six volumes, was published between 1940 and 1967. Towards the end of her life, Libbie accepted that she would not be able to write volumes on the higher mollusks and on the arthropods, as she had proposed. The effort on *Invertebrates* was tremendous: it involved extensive reading of the literature, including articles in German and other languages; then organization; then judgment that required knowledge and experience in comparative anatomy, histology, morphology and physiology; finally, the material had to be presented in clear and concise form.

Libbie Hyman lived to see her magnum opus recognized. Among the honors she received were an honorary doctorate in science from the University of Chicago and gold medals from the Linnean Society of London and from the American Museum of Natural History. It was emphasized that that she was the first woman to receive the latter; Libbie believed that she was a scientist and that her sex was not relevant. The Linnean Society offered to let someone in the American Embassy receive her medal for her. Disliking the idea of a proxy, Hyman flew to London to receive it personally. She was very proud of that recognition.

She died in New York City in 1969 at the age of 80.

Libbie Hyman pursued her scientific interests without undue regard for monetary gain or prestigious titles. She achieved her goal, leaving science a valuable asset. Richard Blackwelder, when professor of zoology at Southern Illinois University, gave her this tribute in 1970: "Miss Hyman won't be widely missed personally because she had few social friends, but scientifically there will be few of us who will leave such a substantial legacy to our successors. No other zoologist in modern times has made such an impression on both Vertebrates and Invertebrates."

# Chapter 11

# Gerty Cori
*Researcher in Biochemistry*

*Marriage is a game best played by two winners.*—American
proverb

   The first American woman to receive a Nobel Prize in physiology or medicine, Gerty Cori formed a highly successful research partnership with her
husband, Carl Cori.
   Gerty Theresa Radnitz was born in Prague on August 15, 1896, the oldest of three daughters of Otto and Martha (Neustadt) Radnitz. Prague was
then part of the Austro-Hungarian empire. The Radnitzes were moderately
rich Jews. Gerty was taught by private tutors until she was 10, when she was
sent to a private school for girls. A maternal uncle who was a professor of
pediatrics at the University of Prague may have played a part in her decision
to become a physician. Lacking the requisite training in Latin , mathematics, physics and chemistry, she attended a gymnasium, from which she graduated in 1914. After passing a very difficult entrance examination, she was
admitted, at 18, to the medical school of the German University of Prague.
(There was also a Czech language branch.)
   One of Gerty's classmates was Carl Cori, whose father was director of
the marine biological station at Trieste, then also part of Austria-Hungary.
As lovers of the outdoors, he and Gerty were enthusiastic mountain climbers
and skiers. She was described as tall and slender, with reddish-brown hair
and brown eyes; she was intelligent, vivacious, quiet and aggressive, and
blessed with a sense of humor. He was handsome, but shy and less likely than
she to make an impression on those who knew him only casually. The couple found that they had many interests in common besides science and outdoor life—literature, music and art, among others. During the Great War,
Carl was drafted to fight in the Austrian Army, but returned to Prague to

**Gerty Cori**
**(Courtesy Archives, Washington University School of Medicine)**

finish his studies. They were married in 1920, the year they obtained their M.D. degrees. Carl was not Jewish. Because of anti–Semitism, Gerty converted to Catholicism.

After graduation, the couple went to Vienna — Gerty to a children's hospital and Carl to a clinic at the university there. The postwar conditions were so bad that Gerty developed xeropthalmia, a condition caused by vitamin A deficiency. (Carl received a free meal a day from the clinic in lieu of pay.)

While still students, the Coris had collaborated on a research project that concerned immunity. Deciding to involve themselves in clinical research rather than medicine, they were looking for a project. They were very eager to leave Vienna. Although they certainly appreciated its cultural advantages, there was little possibility that they could satisfy their professional aspirations there. The desire to emigrate was apparently so great that they had applied to the Dutch government to work for five years among the natives of Java.

However, in 1922, before their applications were processed, Carl was offered a position in Buffalo, New York, on the staff of the New York State Institute for the Study of Malignant Diseases (later Roswell Park Memorial Institute). He was responsible for running the hospital's clinical laboratory, but he also had permission to devote his spare time to research of his own choosing.

Gerty came to Buffalo six months later to work at the same institution. With regard to research, it was in Buffalo that she and Carl began their life-long collaboration on the investigation of carbohydrate metabolism and its regulation. (Carl later turned down an offer that refused him scientific collaboration with his wife.) As he once observed, collaboration requires much give and take on both sides. In this they were successful; although each was ambitious, they did not compete with one another. Especially important, each trusted the other's work.

They became American citizens in 1928. Wanting to know more about their adopted country, they delved into its history and politics. To obtain some familiarity with American literature, they read aloud to one another. (Gerty was a reader; in the years to come, she concentrated on history and biography, while Carl's focus was on poetry, art and archaeology.) During their nine years in Buffalo their friends were not only scientists but people in the world of music. They attended plays in New York City and spent vacations in the Adirondacks and on Cape Cod.

Although there was no criticism concerning their chosen area of research, they were dealing only indirectly with cancer, and they may have had some concern about this, considering that the institution employing them was dedicated to the study of malignant diseases. When Carl was offered the chairmanship of the pharmacology department at Washington University in St. Louis in 1931, he accepted. The nepotism rules then in effect were bent to provide a research position for Gerty in the same department; she would receive only a token salary.

With the effects of the Depression widespread, nepotism rules were common. In fact, the Coris were fortunate to have the opportunity they did. However, the Depression did end, and Gerty served as "research associate" for 13 years — a position hardly commensurate with her abilities towards the latter part of the period. She was granted tenure in 1944 when she became associate professor. In 1947, when Carl was made chairman of the new bio-chemistry department, he promoted his wife to full professor with appropriate salary. When Washington University changed its nepotism laws in the 1950s, both husbands and wives were permitted to work, but in different departments. The chancellor notified Gerty that the new regulation did not apply to her.

In Buffalo, the Coris had used whole animals to follow the fate of ingested sugars. Their choice of this test system probably reflected the work on diabetes and insulin done by Banting and Best in the 1920s. Gerty and Carl also investigated the hormonal control of carbohydrate metabolism.

At Washington University, the couple used tissue preparations rather than intact animals to study specific chemical reactions involved in the breakdown and buildup of glycogen. Glycogen, sometimes referred to as animal starch, is the storage form of glucose, a sugar that provides the body with energy. They succeeded in identifying the enzymes, or catalysts, involved, and isolated the intermediate products formed in the stepwise reactions. In time, this would be considered one of the most brilliant achievements of modern biochemistry. They also elucidated the structure of glycogen.

Through their work, the Coris attracted to their laboratory great scientists from various parts of the world. Some of them would later win Nobel Prizes: Arthur Kornberg, Earl Sutherland, Edwin Krebs, Severo Ochoa, Christian Duve and Luis Leloir. Gerty worked extremely hard, personifying perfection. Her grasp of subject matter was respected by all, and she kept abreast of the burgeoning literature in her field. She once said, "The love for and dedication to one's work seems to me to be the basis of happiness."

In 1936, when she was 40, Gerty gave birth to a son, Thomas, who would in time obtain a Ph.D. in chemistry. She worked in the laboratory until close to the time of delivery. She seems to have been successful in combining her activities at home and at work. The Coris entertained artists, musicians, novelists, business people and scientists in their St. Louis home. They skated, swam, played tennis, tended their garden and went to concerts. They continued to climb mountains — in both the Rockies and the Alps. Gerty's sister, a painter, lived in Italy, and this provided another reason for them to visit Europe.

The pair received numerous honors for their work, the most important being the 1947 Nobel Prize for physiology or medicine. It was awarded jointly for their discovery of the process involved in the catalytic metabolism of glycogen, and to Bernado Houssay of Argentina for his work on the role of the anterior pituitary hormone in the distribution of glycogen in the body and in the control of diabetes. Since the enzyme phosphorylase had played a central part in their achievement, Carl and Gerty generously shared the prize money with some coworkers on the phosphorylase project: Sidney Colwick, Arden Green and Gerhardt Schmidt.

About the time the Coris became Nobel laureates, they learned that Gerty was seriously ill. After she had fainted while skiing in Colorado at 14,000 feet, she was diagnosed with agnogenic myeloid metaplasia. In this rare fatal condition, the bone marrow ceases to produce necessary blood cells. Thus Gerty would be dependent on blood transfusions to combat the inexorable anemia.

She was determined to continue her work. Turning her attention to glycogen-storage disease (described in 1929 and known as von Gierke's disease), she showed in 1952 that an enzyme named glucose-6-phosphatase was missing from the liver of a patient with that disease. This was a significant piece of work and one of which she was justly proud. The work on glycogen storage disease went forward, but her health gradually deteriorated.

The necessary blood transfusions caused side effects. During the period that she was receiving them, much less was known about possible antigen-antibody reactions than is known today. Palliative measures such as removal of the spleen failed. With Carl giving her very strong support, Gerty battled heroically during the 10 years of her progressive illness. She died at home of kidney failure on October 26, 1957. She was 61.

At a memorial service for Gerty Cori, Nobel Laureate Bernardo Houssay paid her this compliment: "She never flagged in the fulfillment of her duties as a wife, mother and scientist, the triple crown that adorned her life."

# Chapter 12

# Helen Taussig
## *Innovative Pediatric Cardiologist*

*Every great advance in science has issued from a new audac-
ity of imagination.* — John Dewey

On November 29, 1944, a one-year-old named Eileen Saxon became the
first human to have a subclavian-to-pulmonary artery anastomosis. The procedure of making an anastomosis between a branch of the aorta and one of
the pulmonary arteries was soon known as the Blalock-Taussig operation,
and it marks the starting point of modern cardiac surgery.

Helen Brooke Taussig was born on May 24, 1898, in Cambridge, Massachusetts, to Frank William Taussig and Edith (Guild) Taussig. She was their
fourth child and third daughter. Frank Taussig, whose father had emigrated
from Bohemia, taught at Harvard University. A distinguished economist, he
later became an adviser to President Woodrow Wilson and was cofounder of
the Harvard Graduate School of Business Administration. Edith Taussig had
studied biology at what was the forerunner of Radcliffe College. She died of
tuberculosis when Helen was 11.

The Taussigs lived in comfort, with summers spent on Cape Cod. They
enjoyed nature and sports. Culture was not neglected, especially music. Helen
was taught at home and then attended a private school for girls, but only
part-time; she had a mild case of tuberculosis and had difficulty in reading.
The latter was because she had dyslexia, a condition little understood in her
day. Encouraged by her father's understanding, she persisted. At school she
even got through such works as *Twelfth Night, Silas Marner* and the autobiography of Benjamin Franklin. She eventually mastered reading, but for her
it remained, with the exception of poetry, a necessity rather than the pleasure it might have otherwise been. Helen's perseverance in overcoming a
handicap became her approach to future problems.

Taussig entered Radcliffe College in 1917, making her mark as a tennis player. At the end of her sophomore year she transferred to the University of California at Berkeley. (Her father had taught summer school there in 1918, and she had accompanied him.) Although very close to her father, she was not in his shadow at Berkeley, as she had been in Cambridge. She graduated from Berkeley in 1921.

Frank Taussig advised his daughter to enter the field of public health. Harvard's School of Public Health did not admit women to their degree program, and this spurred Helen towards entering a medical program elsewhere.

After a six-month tour of Europe with her father and other relatives, she obtained permission to study histology at Harvard Medical School under John Lewis Brener. Then she took Brener's suggestion to study anatomy at Boston University's medical school, which, unlike Harvard, permitted women to study anatomy. At Boston, Alexander Begg had her study an ox heart, which led to her interest in the contraction of cardiac muscle. She devised experiments to demonstrate this, and her work was published in 1925 in the *American Journal of Physiology*. Impressed with her diligence, Begg suggested that she apply to Johns Hopkins Medical School. On the recommendation of noted physiologist Walter Cannon of Harvard, she was admitted to Hopkins in 1924. Cannon noted that he would vote for her entrance to Harvard Medical School if women were admitted, but since they were not, he hoped the more liberal Johns Hopkins would accept her.

Taussig had hoped to work after hours in the physiology laboratory, as she had at Boston University, but this was not allowed, so she tried the heart station at the hospital. It was a good move — the doctor in charge kept her there during her student years and the year following graduation.

In 1928 she began an internship in pediatrics. Her chief was Edward A. Parks, who was organizing specialty clinics at Harriet Lane Home, the children's wing of Johns Hopkins Hospital. In 1930 he put her in charge of the children's heart clinic — at that time primarily concerned with children suffering from rheumatic heart disease. (Due to the availability of penicillin in the 1940s, this disease became rare.) Taussig's appointment to the clinic was the first of many in her career at Hopkins.

She had been with the clinic for less than a year when she experienced a severe loss of hearing. This made it difficult for her to communicate and was especially serious from the standpoint of not being able to rely on the sounds ordinarily picked up by the stethoscope — sounds that were important in diagnosis and prognosis. Hearing aids of the day were of limited help, but Taussig was not going to let another handicap defeat her. She learned lip reading and also how to interpret vibrations made by sound; in other words, she substituted touch for hearing.

The Harriet Lane Home had recently acquired a fluoroscope. Dr. Parks recommended that Taussig use it to study congenital malformations of the heart. It proved very useful for this and other conditions. As the years went by, she learned much about pediatric cardiology; she read the literature; she used autopsy findings; she consulted with Maude Abbott, the Canadian who was an authority on congenital disease. Helen also focused more on physiology than most of her colleagues, who tended to concentrate on structure.

The ductus arteriosus claimed much of her attention. In the fetus, this structure connects the aorta with the pulmonary artery so that some of the pulmonary artery blood bypasses the fetal lung. Until birth, oxygen is supplied from the mother's blood, with oxygen and carbon dioxide exchange taking place in the placenta. Under normal conditions, when the infant breathes, muscular contraction closes the connection and the ductus soon becomes nonfunctional; gaseous exchange takes place in the lungs, which are supplied by the pulmonary artery.

**Helen Taussig**
**(Courtesy National Library of Medicine)**

Some infants are born with the tetralogy of Fallot, described in the nineteenth century by Etienne-Louis Fallot. The disorder includes four structural cardiac defects. The result is that little blood reaches the lung. Taussig observed that the conditions of these infants worsened as the ductus arteriosus closed. Known as "blue babies" because of their skin color, they had air hunger; they lacked energy; their growth was retarded; and many died.

Taussig pondered whether the duct could be kept open; or, better yet, if an artificial duct could be constructed. She came to the conclusion that the prime factor involved was poor oxygenation of the blood.

In 1939, surgeon Robert Gross tied off a child's persistent ductus arteriosus because it was causing excessive blood flow to the lungs. Taussig went to Boston to discuss with Gross the artificial shunt she envisioned for tetralogy of Fallot patients. He was not interested in her idea.

Later she found a surgeon who was. He was Alfred Blalock, a Hopkins medical school graduate who by 1938 was professor of surgery at Vanderbilt University. He had made a name for himself by investigating the nature of surgical shock and then showing that transfusions of blood and plasma could relieve the condition. In 1941 Blalock became chairman of Hopkins' department of surgery.

Taussig's idea prompted Blalock to start experimental work on dogs. First it was shown that constriction of the pulmonary artery could cause a lack of oxygen in the tissues — and this constriction was one of the conditions existing in the tetralogy of Fallot. Then the researchers succeeded in creating an artificial duct between the aorta and subclavian arteries. The work extended over a period of years. In the dog laboratory, a skilled technician named Vivien Thomas performed the operation on more than 200 dogs. Referring to his impression of Helen in 1943, Thomas wrote, "She was tall and slender with a pleasant personality and spoke with a distinct New England accent."

When blue baby Eileen Saxon's clinical condition became critical, Blalock and Taussig believed that their shunt operation could possibly provide relief. It was an immediate success. (Eileen, however, died within a year during another operation.) On Helen's recommendation, an 11-year-old underwent the operation on February 3, 1945. A week later, a nine-year-old followed. In each case, the procedure restored the child's natural color. Now confident that the operation was valid, the two physicians published the results in the *Journal of the American Medical Association.* It was a landmark paper, prompting the development of various surgical techniques involving the heart.

Taussig's clinic was soon drawing patients from many states and countries, some of the patients having nonmedical referrals. It was Helen's task to evaluate each child. The youngsters loved her, and their parents found her considerate and understanding. She tried to keep in touch with the families, ultimately publishing a 28-year followup on all blue babies operated on at Hopkins between 1945 and 1951. Equally attached to Taussig were the many doctors she trained in cardiac cardiology.

Over the years, thousands of blue baby operations were done. Abbott Gaunt, a biology professor, wrote in 1997:

> It is true that I was a tetralogy of Fallot blue baby. In fact, I was the first from New England for which the Blalock-Taussig procedure actually worked. They had lost six previous patients and were not at all sure that I was operable. However, a Viennese doctor [named Richard Bing] was at Hopkins demonstrating his new technique of cardiac catheterization. A young resident, Tom Hall (who is now deceased) convinced Taussig to permit Bing to try his technique on me. On the basis of those findings, she decided to go ahead and is supposed to have remarked, "I think this will be a good one!"
>
> As I was quite young, my memories of Dr. Taussig are sketchy at best. I remember her as a large woman with a very pleasant face. She was hard-of-hearing, and had an electronic stethoscope, which quite fascinated me. As I recall, it was large and chunky by modern methods, but could be switched to broadcast so that others could hear as well.

Baltimore antivivisectionists in 1945 demonstrated against the use of experimental surgical procedures, Later, Taussig testified in Congress about the use of animals in research. She had dogs as pets and worked for the humane treatment of all animals, but believed their sacrifice was sometimes justified.

According to Denton Cooley, who was present as an intern at the Saxon operation and later became one of the world's most eminent heart surgeons, Blalock was sometimes annoyed by Taussig's fiercely protective mother hen–like approach to her young patients. There was often tension between the two principals about the care of patients. One cardiac surgeon reported that after an argument with his colleague, Blalock remarked that if he got to heaven it would be because he got along with Helen Taussig. However, there was mutual respect between them. (Vivien Thomas' book gives the impression that Blalock was not always easy to get along with.)

In addition to her duties in the clinic, Taussig found time to write *Congenital Malformations of the Heart*, published in 1947. The project extended over many years, much of the book being written during Helen's summer vacations on Cape Cod. Rather than analyzing the literature, she emphasized her personal experiences and observations. A revised edition appeared early in the 1960s.

In 1949 Taussig built a home for herself near Johns Hopkins. A gardener, she made sure there was a greenhouse. Amy Clark, who was her housekeeper for some 35 years, made entertaining easy.

In 1958 Taussig participated in an exchange program between the U.S.A. and the U.S.S.R., heading a delegation of six female physicians. Other travels included trips to Europe, South America, Cuba, India, Israel, Japan, Mexico, Puerto Rico, South Africa, China and the Philippines.

In January 1962 she learned through Alois Beuren, whom she had trained in pediatric cardiology, that doctors in Germany were seeing large numbers of children born with marked deformities of the limbs. These findings were of special concern to Helen because of her familiarity with other congenital deformities. Three weeks later, she was on her way to Germany. Widukind Lenz, a physician in Hamburg, had mailed questionnaires to the parents of affected children. He found that many women, when pregnant, had taken Contergan, the trade name for the drug thalidomide. Contergan was used as an over-the-counter sleeping pill. The data collected by Lenz showed that taking Contergan early in pregnancy (while the limb buds are developing) could cause the deformities. Taussig traveled from medical center to center, saw the malformed babies and talked with their parents. A U.S. Army hospital reported that there had been no cases there. This was significant because all drugs used there required approval for use in the United States. Frances Kelsey, a staff physician at the Food and Drug Administration, was withholding permission pending receipt of more information.

Taussig returned home determined to warn of the dangers of thalidomide. She realized that other medications and factors primarily affecting the mother might also affect the fetus — a concept that was not fully appreciated at the time. She pointed out, for example, that an injury to the fetal reproductive system might not become apparent until puberty. She made her findings known at Hopkins, at the University of Maryland, at a session of the American College of Physicians, through articles in *Scientific American* and the *Journal of the American Medical Association,* and through an editorial in *Science.* Senator Estes Kefauver's congressional committee was investigating the need for increased federal control of new drugs, and Taussig testified before this committee, explaining her views on the use of new drugs. She also advocated more liberal abortion laws. (The Supreme Court did not legalize abortion until 1973, and some women who had taken thalidomide were pregnant and unable to have legal abortions in the United States.)

Taussig retired from Johns Hopkins in 1963. It was not until 1959 that she was appointed to the rank of professor of pediatrics. She believed that had she been a man, the promotion would have come long before. But she also said, "If your work is good enough, men will respect you and will grant you what is due you."

After enduring deafness for 30 years, Taussig had surgery that enabled her to hear well. For seven years she enjoyed sounds she had not heard clearly for a very long time. Then she was beset with nerve deafness.

In 1965 she was elected president of the American Heart Association. She wrote 41 scientific articles after retirement. Hopkins made some reparation for the tardy appointment to full professorship: Because her retirement income was relatively small, the university bought her home in Cotuit, Cape Cod, allowing her to live there rent-free. After she died, the house was sold at a profit. With the proceeds, the Helen Taussig Fund was set up to support pediatric research and young physicians in training.

Taussig was killed in an automobile accident in Pennsylvania just before her eighty-eighth birthday.

Helen Taussig received many honors, including the Medal of Freedom from President Lyndon Johnson. There were numerous honorary degrees; the citations of two especially pleased her: "Brilliant daughter of a brilliant father, her scientific investigations have helped to save countless children from death or lives of crippling pain" (from Harvard University); and "You have brought to medicine simplicity, kindness and compassion as only a complete woman can" (from Goucher College).

# Chapter 13

# Barbara McClintock
## *Geneticist*

*But in science the credit goes to the man who convinces the world...* — Francis Darwin-1914

This is the story of a woman whose confidence in her results prevailed despite years of nonrecognition on the part of most of her scientific peers.

Eleanor McClintock was born on June 16, 1902, in Hartford Connecticut, the youngest of three daughters of Thomas Henry McClintock and Sara (Handy) McClintock. Her father was a homeopathic physician and her mother a *Mayflower* descendant who encouraged marriage rather than higher education for her daughters. When her husband's practice was bringing in very little, she taught piano to help the family finances. She was also an amateur painter and poet.

By the time Eleanor was four months old, her parents decided that the name Barbara better suited their offspring, and they made the change. They had wanted a boy, and one did arrive when Barbara was two. When the burden of raising four young children became too much for Sara McClintock, Barbara was sometimes sent to an aunt and uncle in Massachusetts. The uncle peddled fish, first from a wagon, then from a truck, and Barbara liked to go with him. He taught her to repair machinery and to love nature. (Later in life, she was mechanically inclined.) Her father gave her boxing gloves when she was four, and she came to enjoy ice skating, roller skating, bicycling and basketball with boys.

Although Mrs. McClintock may not have approved of such masculine pursuits for her daughter, she did not restrict them. Barbara later claimed that there was coldness between her and her mother; she also credited that parent with being supportive. Both father and mother appear to have been unusually permissive for their day. Uninterested in playing with girls and not

**Barbara McClintock**
**(Courtesy Cold Spring Harbor Laboratory Archives)**

completely accepted by boys, Barbara kept to herself, reading and thinking. She appears to have been an introverted and independent child.

The family moved to Flatbush, New York, in 1908. Summers were spent at Long Beach. During her school days, Barbara displayed great intensity with regard to some situations — music lessons, for example. This characteristic of total absorption in the subject at hand would distinguish her professional career. While a student at Erasmus High School, she became interested in science, and by the time of her graduation in 1919, she was determined to enter Cornell University's College of Agriculture, where she would not have to pay tuition.

Mrs. McClintock did not approve of her daughter's plan; she feared that Barbara would become a professor. However, when Dr. McClintock returned from overseas service during World War I, the decision was made that Barbara would go to Ithaca.

She thoroughly enjoyed Cornell; she not only made friends, but was elected president of the freshmen women. Most of these friends were Jewish; one of them, Laura Hobson, would write *Gentleman's Agreement*. Although invited to join a sorority, Barbara declined because she disliked any kind of discrimination. Just over 5 feet and weighing 90 pounds, she was an attractive young woman. She had many dates during the first two years. After taking a course in harmony, she joined a jazz group as their banjo player.

A course in genetics sparked McClintock's interest in the subject; eventually it would become her consuming interest. She also decided that the institution of marriage was not for her. In 1923, she became a graduate student in the botany department, with a minor in genetics and zoology. Her major was in cytology, a subject concerned with the microscopic study of cells. Her thesis advisor was Lester Sharp, the author of *An Introduction to Cytology*. After receiving the Ph.D. in 1927, Barbara remained at Cornell as an instructor.

When McClintock was a student, it was known that the nucleus of the cell had chromosomes, the number varying with the species; that the chromosomes carried entities called genes; and that these entities were involved in inheritance. Her test material was corn, or maize, the botanical name of which is *Zea mays*. This was useful because genetic changes were readily observed in the color and consistency of individual kernels. On the other hand, growing corn and experimentally controlling its pollination required much time and effort: The young plants required constant watering, and so on. Another important drawback was the length of the growth cycle — it took a year to produce a new generation. McClintock became an expert at growing and breeding maize because she realized its importance in her research.

Her special expertise was in the cytology involved. She had an unusual ability to observe microscopic details unnoticed by most cytologists. By modifying a staining method that used the dye carmine, she had discovered how to identify each of the ten chromosomes of *Zea mays*. By 1927 she was planning an experiment that would engage all her capabilities.

It was then accepted (see Chapter 2), but not proven, that what are now called genes are located on the chromosomes within the nucleus, and that during the process of meiosis, maternal and paternal chromosomes can exchange parts. Meiosis is the process of cell division by which the chromosome number of a male and a female cell is halved prior to the formation of a new entity.

McClintock's aim was to demonstrate that the microscopic crossing-over between two like chromosomes was correlated with the production of kernels displaying certain characteristics. The cross formed by the two chromosomes involved can be seen microscopically at a certain stage of meiosis.

McClintock knew exactly how to proceed, but she needed help. She was fortunate to find Harriet Creighton, a graduate of Wellesley College, who was enrolled in the Ph.D. program in botany at Cornell.

One chromosome of maize had a distinctive microscopic appearance — a prominent knob at one end and an additional length of chromatin at the other. The latter was due to chromosome 9's interchange with chromosome 8. Chromatin is chromosomal material that looks like dispersed clumps of stainable material. This artificially bred chromosome was associated with purple, waxy kernels.

The two women planted waxy, purple kernels from the special strain McClintock had selected. In summer, they fertilized with pollen from a plant of the same strain, but with kernels neither waxy nor purple. In the fall, some plants had waxy, purple kernels; some had neither waxy nor purple; some were either waxy or purple. Microscopic examination showed that either the knob or the elongated tip of chromosome 9 had actually exchanged places; no longer did every elongated chromosome have a knob — there were elongated chromosomes minus knobs and chromosomes with knobs but minus elongated tips. The results were such that the women could report: "The foregoing evidence points to the fact that cytological crossing-over occurs and is accompanied by the expected types of genetic crossing-over."

Their work was published just in time to prevent their being scooped. When Thomas Hunt Morgan, distinguished geneticist and Nobel Prize winner to-be (see Chapter 2), came to Cornell from Columbia University as a visiting lecturer, he talked with Barbara. After looking at the preliminary data obtained by her and Harriet Creighton, he insisted that they publish it without waiting for another year's crop of corn. He even wrote then and there to the editor of *Proceedings of the National Academy of Sciences* to expect the article in two weeks. It arrived on July 7, 1931, and was published the following month. According to Keller's book about McClintock, Morgan was aware that Curt Stern, in Germany, was working to present the same information with regard to *Drosophila*, the fruit fly. With that test system, a new generation can be produced every ten days or so, and it appeared likely that Stern would have conclusive results before Barbara's next generation of maize matured. (Stern did publish, but after McClintock.)

Thanks to McClintock's generosity, Harriet Creighton was officially the first author. Colleagues were aware, however, that greater credit was due the second author, and the paper established her reputation as a top-flight geneticist.

Cornell had other geneticists of note; for example: Rollins Emerson, the department head; Marcus Rhoades, Barbara's friend and admirer who could explain her work to some who found her writing hard to understand; and George Beadle, a future Nobel Laureate. Barbara enjoyed their intellectual companionship; they respected her knowledge and genius. She worked very hard and systematically — physically, as she took care of her corn stocks, and mentally, as she spent hours at her microscope. To relax, she played tennis regularly and found time to visit at the home of her physician friend, Esther Parker. But it was research that dominated her life.

A time came when McClintock was no longer content to remain an instructor. Since there was little likelihood that Cornell would appoint a woman to a senior faculty position, she began to look elsewhere. In 1931, the National Research Council awarded her a fellowship for the next two years. She was fortunate, for this was a Depression year, and support was hard to come by. Retaining her laboratory at Cornell, she also worked at the University of Missouri and at the California Institute of Technology.

The summer of 1931, spent at the University of Missouri, proved exceptionally profitable to McClintock. A former Cornell associate, Lewis Stadler, was there studying the mutagenic effects of X-rays. It had been discovered only four years earlier that X-rays can produce mutation, and Barbara was very keen to learn as much as possible about the matter. The procedure was to fertilize kernels of plants having recessive genes with radiated pollen grains of plants carrying dominant genes. McClintock's task was to identify the small microscopic changes in the chromosomes induced by exposure to X-rays. This work spurred her interest in ring chromosomes, small fragments related to variegation in the corresponding plants.

At Cal Tech she felt at home because Morgan and Beadle had moved there. While at Pasadena, she became interested in a small body at the end of chromosome 6, adjacent to where the chromosome attaches to the nucleolus. (The nucleolus is indirectly involved in the synthesis of protein.) After intense study, McClintock concluded that the area in question, which she termed nucleolar organizer (NOR), is required for the development of the nucleolus.

In 1933, Morgan, Emerson and Stadler recommended McClintock for a Guggenheim Foundation Scholarship, which was awarded. For a short time, she studied with Richard Goldschmid at the Kaiser Wilhelm Institute in Berlin. Apparently the Hitler regime was more than she could stand, and she was back in Ithaca before the year was out.

McClintock's financial situation was now precarious; despite the professional esteem of her peers, she would soon be without support for the coming year. She had little interest in money, but she needed enough to live on, and this included maintaining a car (she traveled 100 miles every three days, visiting her plots.) Morgan appealed to the Rockefeller Foundation to finance her, noting that such an award would be a contribution to the field of genetics. He credited her with being the most able person in the world in what he called the narrow category of the cytology of maize genetics. Emerson made it clear that Cornell's Department of Botany did not wish to reappoint her because her interest was entirely in research and because she was not wholly successful in teaching undergraduates.

The Rockefeller Foundation awarded Emerson a grant to pay McClintock's salary while she worked in his laboratory at Cornell for a year, beginning October 1, 1934. Although the grant was renewed for a second year, Barbara was not happy as a post-doctoral fellow. From the beginning of her career, she had published regularly, but for 1936, no publications were listed.

Stadler wanted McClintock to work with him in Columbia, Missouri. Pressed by him, the University of Missouri hired her as assistant professor. She stayed there for five years, focusing her investigations on chromosome formations made by the rejoining of fragments. During this period, the Genetics Society of America elected her vice president in 1939.

From the beginning, she felt like an outsider. In June 1941, she asked the dean about her likelihood of promotion. She was told that if Dr. Stadler resigned, there would be no place for her at the University of Missouri. At that point she left, first requesting a leave of absence without pay.

In December, 1941, Milislav Demerec became Director of Genetics at the Carnegie Institution in Cold Spring Harbor, New York. As a geneticist, he knew Barbara and was familiar with her work. He now found her a one-year position in his outfit. It became permanent after a few months.

Astonishingly, McClintock had had doubts about accepting the position — an opportunity to receive a permanent salary, provisions for her research and a home. To be sure, she was not on a university campus, but when she had been, she had found academic regulations confining.

The move proved to be a good one. By 1944, McClintock's reputation was such that she was elected to the National Academy of Sciences and also elected president of the Genetics Society of America.

The same year, George Beadle invited her to his laboratory at Stanford University. He needed help in identifying the chromosomes of *Neurospora*, the mold he used as a test system. McClintock went and, according to Beadle, in two months did more to elucidate the cytology of *Neurospora* than other cytological geneticists had done with all forms of mold. Years later, when recalling the problem, Barbara emphasized that for a time she was lost, not seeing things, not integrating. Worried, she took a walk on the campus, then sat on a bench overhung with eucalyptus trees. She needed to think. After half an hour, she knew what to do. Her genius, her past experience and reflection about the problem at hand served her well — and would again serve her in integrating new facts.

For the next six years, she studied what is now called transposition. Her research involved plants with repeated cycles of chromosome breakage. She observed that in them, gene activity was being systematically turned on and off. After very careful study of many generations, McClintock decided that there existed what she termed controlling elements, and that the latter seemed able to move from site to site on different chromosomes of *Zea mays*, and these "jumping genes," or transposons, had the potential to act as biologic switches.

McClintock regularly sent progress reports to the Carnegie Institution; in 1950, she described transposition in *Proceedings of the National Academy of Sciences*. The following year, she presented her work at the Annual Cold Spring Harbor Symposium. Apparently both were difficult to understand and assess. Subsequent seminars and publication in 1953 in *Genetics* did not improve the situation.

Great was her disappointment, but her research at Cold Spring Harbor went forward, except for two winters spent in Central and South America when she trained Latin American cytologists to identify strains of corn.

For many years, her work remained largely disregarded. The science of genetics was now intertwined with that of molecular biology, and young students in genetics were unfamiliar with methods that involved cytogenetics. James Darnell and co-authors of the 1990 edition of *Molecular Cell Biology* suggest what happened: "Barbara McClintock discovered the first *mobile elements* in corn (maize) over 40 years ago. She characterized agents that could move into and back out of genes, altering genetic activity during the process, but these elements were not understood in molecular terms until very recently."

McClintock had a lifelong habit of keeping up with the literature in and related to her field. In 1960, she was encouraged by work by Jacques Monod and Francois Jacob of the Pasteur Institute in Paris, later Nobel Laureates. Their paper described regulator and operator genes in bacteria. Her work was not cited. She then wrote "Some Parallels Between Gene Control Systems in Maize and in Bacteria" for the *American Naturalist*. It failed to convince those she wanted to convert. However, in 1961, at the Cold Spring Harbor Symposium, the papers of which were published, Monod stated: "Long before regulator and operator genes were revealed in bacteria, the extensive and penetrating work of McClintock ... had revealed the existence in maize, of two classes of genetic 'controlling elements' whose specific mutual relationships are closely comparable with those of the regulator and operator." Transposition was not mentioned.

Transposable elements were discovered in bacteria; then it was found that they were involved in, for example, inherited birth defects and resistance to antibiotics. With recombinant DNA technology, they could be used in a variety of ways. It was clear the transposition was not limited exclusively to *Zea mays*; it was a common occurrence.

At long last, McClintock received the recognition she deserved. In 1980 and 1981, eight major awards were bestowed on her. Evelyn Fox Keller, a scientist, wrote a good biography, published in 1983.

In 1983, Barbara McClintock, at age 81, was the sole recipient of the Nobel Prize for physiology or medicine. The Nobel Committee described her work on transposition as "one of the two great discoveries of our times in genetics." (The other was the structure of DNA, elucidated by Watson and Crick.)

She publicly thanked the Carnegie Institution, pointing out that elsewhere she might have been fired because she was not publishing and because no one was accepting her work. "When you're right, you don't care," she said. "You just know, sooner or later, it will come out in the wash, but you may have to wait some time."

She continued her research until she died. She was well off at the time of her death, thanks to her prizes. She often traveled to South America to pursue problems arising with regard to the experimental cultivation of maize. She became proficient in Spanish. Very late in life, she changed her workday from 12 to 8 hours. Her colleagues considered her a mystic. She died on September 2, 1991, at 90.

To some, Barbara McClintock's circumstances may seem tragic. How much of her trouble was due to her own making cannot be judged. She did note that she had led "a very, very interesting and satisfying life," which should probably be taken on its word.

# Chapter 14

# Virginia Apgar
*Anesthesiologist and Teratologist*

> *How doth the little busy bee*
> *Improve each shining hour,*
> *And gather honey all the day*
> *From each opening flower!*
>
> — Isaac Watts

Virginia Apgar was an industrious anesthesiologist whose contributions strengthened neonatology; later she became an ardent advocate for the prevention of birth defects.

Virginia Apgar, better known as Ginny, was born on June 7, 1909, in Tenafly, New Jersey, the daughter of Charles and Helen (Clarke) Apgar. The former was a salesman with innovative ideas. Virginia had four older brothers, the oldest of whom had died before her birth. The family had little money to spare, but the parents instilled in their children curiosity and a love of learning. Charles, for example, studied the stars with his own telescope; family members read aloud to each other; they all played musical instruments and were known to give impromptu concerts. They were described as a group that never sat down, and Virginia followed the family pattern. It is not surprising that her activities at Westfield High School included orchestra, debate club, Greek, higher mathematics, stamp collecting, basketball, tennis and track. She graduated in 1925.

She enrolled as a premedical student at Mount Holyoke College, the institution whose reputation in science had been enhanced by the efforts of Cornelia Clapp. To support herself, Virginia won a scholarship and had odd jobs such as opening the library every day at 7:15 in the morning. Her whirlwind existence continued, and she admitted that medical school seemed easy after her senior year in college. She graduated from Mount Holyoke in 1929.

Four years later, she obtained her M.D. from Columbia University

Virginia Apgar
(Courtesy Mount Holyoke College Archives and Special Collections, South Hadley Massachusetts)

College of Physicians and Surgeons. Her grades were high enough to gain her election to Alpha Omega Alpha, the medical honor society.

With the intention of becoming a surgeon, Apgar completed two years of training in that field at Columbia's Presbyterian Hospital. An episode that occurred during that period gives insight into her integrity. After one of her patients had died postoperatively, permission for an autopsy could not be obtained. Fearing that she had inadvertently made a serious error during the operation, Virginia decided to investigate herself. When the body was in the morgue, she reopened the operative incision, finding that she had indeed caused the mishap she had suspected. She immediately informed the chief surgeon.

Much as she wanted to practice surgery, she knew that it was risky from the financial standpoint, especially since the public was not used to women surgeons. She had borrowed money for medical school, and had little in reserve. At the suggestion of a surgery professor, she decided to enter the field of anesthesiology, at the time relatively new for physicians. Nurses customarily gave anesthesia, but there were indications that as surgical techniques became more extensive, a deeper knowledge of anesthesiology would be beneficial.

Apgar first worked under Ralph Waters at the University of Wisconsin's medical school, then under Emery Rovensteine at Bellevue Hospital in New York City. The fiftieth physician to be board-certified in anesthesiology, in 1938, she was appointed clinical director of the Department of Anesthesiology at Columbia University.

In the course of the next 11 years, her department grew until it was scheduling as many as 65 operations a day; there were 10 certified anesthesiologists; with 22 residents to train, teaching was an important function. Most important were the patients, and Virginia enjoyed contact with them — for instance, it was known that this large, energetic woman with blue eyes once carried a little boy up nine flights of stairs because she knew that he was afraid of elevators. The success of the department grew, and, by 1949, Apgar was a full professor.

That year, she withdrew from administrative work to spend full time in the delivery room, where she assisted at deliveries, gave anesthesia to mothers in labor and revived newborns. During her tenure there, there were thousands of deliveries. She kept wondering who was responsible for the newborn — the obstetrician or the pediatrician. The latter was seldom present until later, while the former was often too occupied with the condition of the mother to give immediate attention to the infant. She realized that some problems could be avoided if they were noted immediately after birth.

She began to record all the signs about newborns that could be observed without special equipment and that helped to spot those that required emergency help. After much study, she devised a scoring system to predict which infants would need special attention in the first minutes and hours of life. The system measured heart rate, respiration, muscle tone, reflexes and color, with checks being made at 1 and 5 minutes after birth. Each sign had a value from 0 through 2. A score of 7-10 was satisfactory; a score of 4-7 indicated the necessity of careful watching; a score of less than 4 required emergency measures such as artificial respiration. Virginia presented her concept at a special meeting of the International Anesthesia Research Society in 1952. Known as the Apgar Score, the system became standard procedure in hospitals in the United States and many other countries. Medical students memorized the procedure as:

A for appearance
P for pulse
G for grimace
A for activity
R for respiration

A physician once remarked that every baby born in a modern hospital anywhere in the world was seen first through the eyes of Virginia Apgar.

Granted a sabbatical leave from Columbia, Apgar spent the time at Johns Hopkins pursuing a master's degree in public health. During that time, she was approached about taking a position with the National Foundation–March of Dimes. The agency's focus had been on poliomyelitis. However, in 1959, it was clear that the success of the Salk vaccine (soon to be followed by the Sabin vaccine) dictated a change of focus on the part of the March of Dimes. A new area of investigation would be birth defects, and Virginia would be in charge. She accepted, taking on a new career direction in middle age. She told a newspaper reporter that one factor in her decision was Columbia's mandatory retirement age of 65, and that she definitely did not want to retire then.

For the remaining years of her life, Apgar expended her energy on behalf of congenital malformations. She traveled all over the world, educating the public about the necessity for research into the prevention of birth defects. Thanks mainly to her efforts, the annual income of the National Foundation increased from $19 to $46 million. To capitalize on what was already known about the prevention of birth defects, she made numerous speeches and wrote many articles for both physicians and the laity. Between 1965-71, she taught classes in teratology, the study of serious malformations, at Cornell University Medical College. This was the first time the subject was taught as a medical subspecialty.

In 1972, she authored with Joan Beck *Is My Baby All Right?: A Guide to Birth Defects.* It emphasized good prenatal care and such measures as testing for rubella. Down's syndrome, cystic fibrosis, sickle cell anemia, clubfoot and many other conditions were covered in detail. There was an interesting chapter on genetic counseling, from which the following is quoted: "Just how much encouragement and help a genetic counselor can give prospective parents depends on how big a role defective genes play in causing the particular disorder about which they are concerned, how much geneticists know about its patterns of inheritance and what medical help is available." The author noted that if a very serious disorder were diagnosed, the pregnancy might, under some circumstances, be terminated. (As mentioned elsewhere, the Supreme Court liberalized the abortion laws in 1973.) On the other hand, if the fetus did not have the suspected condition, the parents would be spared unnecessary worry, at least about that particular child.

Always the student, Apgar went to Hopkins again in 1972 to study genetics. During the last year of her life, she taught the subject at Hopkins School of Public Health.

She had many interests besides her profession. Music was a major part of her life; she belonged to amateur performers groups and constructed three instruments — violin, viola, and cello — all of which she played expertly. She was a stamp collector, photographer, fisherman and gardener. Late in life she took up golf and flying.

She found time to care for her mother, who lived close to her in Tenafly. She also served as a member of the board of trustees of her alma mater, Mount Holyoke College. A Methodist, she became, in 1965, a member-at-large of the Methodist Board of Hospitals and Homes.

In the last years of her life, Virginia suffered from progressive cirrhosis of the liver. However, she remained active until her death on August 7, 1974.

Virginia Apgar would no doubt be pleased to know how much the care of the premature infant has advanced since her day and how much molecular biology is contributing to medical genetics. And the Apgar Score remains her monument; it is still determined throughout the world on every infant born in a medical setting.

During her life, she received much recognition, but perhaps the greatest honor she received was posthumous: In 1994, a 20-cent postage stamp was issued in her honor.

Contending that "women are liberated from the time they leave the womb," she worried little about sex discrimination, her philosophy being, "If you're good, you're good!" And she was good.

# Chapter 15

# Maria Goeppert Mayer
## *Theoretical Physicist*

*Physics tries to discover the pattern of events which controls
the phenomena we observe.* — James Hopwood Jeans

A Nobel Laureate, Maria Goeppert Mayer was a physicist of first rank.
She was also an immigrant. Unlike most of the women previously discussed
in this book, she married and had a family.

Maria was born on June 28, 1906, in Kattowitz, Upper Silesia, now part
of Poland, but then a province of Germany. Her parents were Friedrich Goeppert, a pediatrician and professor at the University of Göttingen, and Maria
(Wolff) Goeppert, a former school teacher. The couple had no other children.

Because a German professor commanded great prestige and received a
good salary, Maria led a privileged existence. Her father inspired her to use
her mind, taking his young daughter on science walks that involved quarry
fossils and forest plants; at seven, she was provided with filters he made for
her to watch a solar eclipse. Frau Goeppert, highly regarded as a hostess and
musician, did not insist that her daughter follow the usual feminine pursuits
of the day. Her husband believed that women stifled inquisitiveness and daring in their offspring. Although his wife was naturally protective, she let
Friedrich Goeppert have his way. Thus young Maria, who adored her father,
was greatly influenced by his desire that she become something other than a
housewife. She knew that she was expected to acquire training or education
that would enable her to earn a living so that she would not be dependent on
marriage.

Maria was eight when the Great War began. Food donated by Quakers
saved her from malnutrition, but her parents, like Gerty Cori, suffered from
the devastation in postwar Europe.

In her teens, Maria excelled in mathematics and languages. In 1921, she entered a small private school run by suffragists to prepare girls for the university. It closed two years later because of the serious inflation that followed the war. Although Maria lacked the usual three years of formal preparation, she took and passed the abitur, or university entrance examination, being admitted to the University of Göttingen in the spring of 1924. (Gerty Cori, profiled herein, remembered the abitur as one of the stiffest examinations she ever took.)

At the time, the university was noted for its department of mathematics, and faculty member David Hilbert was a mathematician of great renown. A growing number of distinguished physicists were becoming attracted to Göttingen, and the physics department, with Max Born, James Franck and Werner Heisenberg, would outshine the mathematics department. Maria, with blue eyes and blond hair, was regarded not only as exceptionally beautiful, but as a good student. Her socially prominent family was on equal footing with the great professors, some of whom she looked on as friends or near-relatives. Initially she had intended to study mathematics, but in 1927 she changed to physics after attending a seminar by Born.

After Friedrich Goeppert's death that year, she decided to take the Ph.D. in quantum mechanics, the new science evolving at Göttingen. This would enable her to state at a later date that on her father's side, she was the seventh straight generation of university professors. In 1928, she won a government fellowship to study for a term at Girton College, Cambridge. Among other benefits gained from the experience, her pronunciation of English improved.

Quantum theory deals with the emission and absorption of energy by molecules, atoms and elementary particles. Embracing Einstein's theory that mass is related to energy, it holds that energy is emitted and absorbed in tiny, discrete amounts, not in a continuous manner, as previously thought. An individual unit of energy, called a quantum, exhibits wavelike properties that may be identified from the spectral characteristics of the element represented by the atom. Quantum mechanics is the final mathematical formulation of the quantum theory — for example, it can show the probability of finding a particle at a given point in space.

During her training under Max Born in Göttingen, Goeppert became friendly with such luminaries as Robert Oppenheimer, Enrico Fermi, Max Delbruck and Victor Weisskopt. She seldom associated with women; according to her, it was enjoyable to be with the boys. She had many suitors among the boys.

One visiting scientist changed her life. He was Joseph Mayer, from the University of California at Berkeley. One of Frau Goeppert's boarders, he was handsome and moderately well off. He found Maria lovely and the brightest girl he had ever met. When they became engaged, she had thoughts of leaving physics. but Joe was determined she continue, and from the time of their marriage, he never withdrew his encouragement. She was awarded the Ph.D. in March 1930 with her doctoral committee consisting of three men who had won, or would win, Nobel Prizes. Her dissertation showed the probability that an orbiting electron would emit two quantum units of light as it jumps to an orbit closer to the nucleus.

Joe had an appointment at Johns Hopkins University as assistant professor of chemistry, and the couple moved to Baltimore. As had Gerty Cori, Maria had to contend with nepotism laws — a university was not likely to hire a professor's wife, especially during the Depression, and Hopkins was no different. However, some members of the physics department allowed her to work with them as a volunteer — after all, her mentors were Hilbert, Franck and Born. She also collaborated with Joe and did some teaching and thesis supervision. Her research during her years in Baltimore involved theoretical chemistry. Not listed in the university catalogue, she still managed to have some publications. She noted later that she would have fought back if she had had to, but her chief concern was to learn, to teach and to work. Money was apparently secondary, and she found a way to satisfy her intellectual desires. At the same time, she was ambitious, and intended to make a name for herself professionally. A visit from her mother brightened Maria's life, and she also returned to Germany to work with Born for some summers.

**Maria Goeppert Mayer**
**(Courtesy University of Chicago Library)**

As the Hitler regime became more entrenched in Germany, the Mayers opened their home to some refugees. Intensely proud of her German heritage, Maria at first looked on Hitler as an aberration and actually had trust in Hermann Goering; she slowly realized she was mistaken. She became an American citizen in 1933. However, by dividing her loyalties, World War II caused her much anguish.

There was additional conflict in her life. Daughter Marianne was born in 1933 and son Peter in 1938. Encouraged by Joe, she spent as much time as possible in the laboratory, where she wanted to be. She would note: "There is an emotional strain due to conflicting allegiances, that to science and that to the children, who, after all, need a mother. I have had this experience in full measure."

In 1938, Joe lost his position at Hopkins. He was hired by Columbia University and worked in the department of chemistry under Harold Urey, Nobel Laureate in 1934. He would be Joe's mentor for years to come. He also gave Maria a minor teaching position, an office and the title of Lecturer in Chemistry. She used the latter in *Statistical Mechanics*, a text she and Joe wrote together. The first edition appeared in 1940 and was considered a classic. She had been turned down when she applied for a position in the physics department.

The Mayers moved in 1940 to Leonia, New Jersey, where a small colony of celebrated scientists was forming. Marianne and Peter had fond memories of their mother reading and singing to them. (Maria was a lover of poetry.) Fermi taught them Italian history; Urey told them about dinosaurs; they knew Edmund Teller as a ping pong player. The adult Mayers were noted for their competitive bridge playing and partying; both were chain smokers and Maria was a social drinker.

Offered a part time position in 1941 at Sarah Lawrence College, she designed an interdisciplinary course that unified astronomy, chemistry and physics. Although noted for her organization in running her home, she must sometimes have been overwhelmed: she once drove her husband to the Leonia railway station in her bathrobe, then drove on 20 miles to Sarah Lawrence, in Bronxville, New York, in the same attire.

Urey recruited her in the spring of 1942 to work on the Manhattan Project, in which the atomic bomb was being developed in secret. She enjoyed the work, received a salary and soon had others working under her direction. However, when she made it clear that she would not work on Saturdays and when the children were sick, she was assigned to a secondary project. Joe was doing weapons research, which kept him away from home most of the time. In 1945, he went to the South Pacific. At the same time, Maria spent a month at Los Almos, New Mexico, involved with research under Teller on the hydrogen bomb.

With the defeat of Japan, the group at Leonia moved to Chicago in 1946. Joe became a full professor at the University of Chicago and Maria an associate professor without pay. She accepted the situation because she was in the company of Fermi, Franck, Teller, Urey and others she looked up to and who respected her as a scientist. Hired by her own former graduate student, she became also a senior physicist at the nearby Argonne National Laboratory.

It was in Chicago that Maria did the work that brought her fame. Wartime research on the atom bomb had produced much knowledge about isotopes and radioactivity. Mayer began a project with Teller involving the origin of the elements. Both were impressed that certain elements were stable and abundant. She learned that previously a Göttingen professor had investigated the matter, but had not solved it.

Teller went on to other investigations, but she continued the work. Aided by data obtained from the use of the cyclotron, she made a systematic investigation of all available information. She found that all the abundant and stable isotopes comprised a series of "magic numbers"—2, 8, 20, 28, 50, 82 — numbers that represented either neutrons or protons, the building blocks of the nucleus. The term "magic" was first used by Eugene Wigner who would receive half of the 1963 Nobel Prize for Physics.

Current thought at the time favored a theory postulated by Niels Bohr to explain the structure of the nucleus. Mayer considered instead a shell theory that had evolved in the 1930s but had been dropped. The shell model describes spherical layers, or orbits, in which protons and neutrons are allowed to move. It did not explain how the protons held together, how they interact with one another and with the neutrons. She did however, present her findings, minus a theoretical explanation, by publishing in *Physical Review* in 1948.

Maria was also enjoying the social life in Chicago. The Mayers lived among other faculty members in the city's south side in a house with six fireplaces and a glass porch where Maria could grow her orchids. It also had a library on the second floor and a billiard room on the third. Outside there was room for large vegetable and flower gardens. Every Christmas, Maria and Joe entertained over 100 senior scientists who found a 12-foot Christmas tree decorated German-style. Maria, like her mother, loved to give elegant parties. Not usually interested in politics, she became a dove with regard to the Vietnam War. Joe was a hawk.

Her greatest triumph came inadvertently. Fermi was in her office one day, discussing nuclear structure. (He disliked having smokers in his own office, and Maria usually smoked.) On the way out to answer a long distance call, he said, "Incidentally, is there any evidence of spin-orbit coupling?" (Spin-orbit coupling is the simultaneous orbiting and spinning of electrons in their movement around the nucleus, some moving clockwise, some counterclockwise.) Mayer made a calculation that assumed that spin-orbit coupling existed within the nucleus. Unlike the situation with the electrons, which rotate in orbits beyond the nucleus, it was very strong. She recognized immediately that a measured spin of a nuclear particle can correspond to either one or two different orbits. She wrote later:

> One can then picture the building of the structure of the nucleus as gradual filling up of single-particle orbits by neutrons and protons, in the same way as electrons build the atom.... In this scheme, the magic numbers should correspond to closed shells; that is, they should indicate the boundaries where one level is filled and the next level is appreciably higher.... The larger

magic numbers all occur at the places where spin-orbit coupling has its greatest effect.

Eugene Wigner and David Inglis had once thought of relating spin-orbit coupling to nuclear particles, but had shown nothing conclusive. Mayer stated, "Only if one had lived with the data as long as I, could one answer [Fermi's question] with 'Yes, of course, and that will explain everything.'" (This is reminiscent of Pasteur's aphorism that in the fields of observation, chance favors only the mind that is prepared.)

At Joe's urging, Maria submitted her work in December 1949 for publication. It appeared in the April 1950 *Physical Review*, with the title "Nuclear Configuration in the Spin-Orbit Coupling Model, I, Empirical Evidence and II Theoretical Considerations." Fermi refused to be a co-author, explaining that he was already famous; with his name on the paper, the work would be attributed to him rather than to Mayer.

Hans Jensen of Heidelberg, with two colleagues, had simultaneously arrived at the same conclusion as Mayer, and his paper arrived only two days after Maria's. She decided that this confirmation of her work would make its acceptance more likely. The "Beauty of Göttingen" became "Madonna of the Onion" when she described shells as "built up like an onion in layers."

In the summer of 1950, the United States Department of State sponsored a visit by the Mayers to Germany. On this occasion, Maria met Jensen. Later Bohr invited both to Copenhagen. They got along so well that Jensen suggested they write a book together on the shell model. She agreed, but it turned out that she wrote four-fifths of the work. *Elementary Theory of Nuclear Shell Structure* was published by Wiley in 1955, with Maria as senior author. It was dedicated "to our most patient and most constructive critic, Joseph E. Mayer."

The following year, Maria suddenly lost the hearing in her left ear. Fermi had died, which meant that fewer good students came to Chicago. Other atomic scientists had moved on; when Urey took a position at a new branch of the University of California at San Diego, he made offers to the Mayers. They moved to La Jolla in 1960, with Maria, then 53, taking her first full-time, paid faculty position, a full professorship.

The year before, Marianne had married an astrophysicist. Maria would have liked her daughter to follow in her footsteps. This did not happen; however, having a scientist son-in-law pleased Maria.

A short time after she arrived in California, she had a serious cerebral hemorrhage. Her left arm was paralyzed, her walk slowed down and her speech was blurred. She never really recovered her health.

In 1963, the Nobel Prize for Physics ($51,158) was awarded as follows: half to Eugene Wigner, then at Princeton University, via Göttingen; and half jointly to Maria Goeppert Mayer and Hans Jensen. According to Joe Mayer, the latter half was given "for the *explanation* based on the single assumption that spin-orbit coupling (which was assumed to be very small) was prodigious, especially in heavy elements."

Joe accompanied her to Stockholm. Max Born sent flowers to their hotel. Maria, then 57, wore a green brocade dress at the ceremony and a long red chiffon gown at the king's banquet. Once during the festivities, she saw tears in Joe's eyes.

Maria received many honors besides the Nobel Prize. She also became a grandmother and saw Peter, an economist, represent the eighth generation of university professors in her family.

In 1968, Maria required a pacemaker. She continued to work in the laboratory as long as possible, but was less productive. She died on February 20, 1972.

After her death, Robert Sachs, a physicist who had been a student of Maria's, summed up her professional life:

> Winning the [Nobel Prize] had its beginning in her early exposure to an intense atmosphere of science, both at home and in the surrounding university community, a community providing her with the opportunity to follow her inclinations and to develop her remarkable talents under the guidance of the great teachers and scholars of mathematics and physics. Throughout her full and gracious life, her science continued to be the theme about which her activities were centered, and it culminated in her major contribution to the understanding of the structure of the atomic nucleus, the spin-orbit coupling shell model of the nucleus.

# Chapter 16

# Grace Hopper
## *Pioneer Computer Programmer and Naval Officer*

*Where there is no vision, the people perish.* — Proverbs 29:18

Grace Hopper's first career was in college teaching. World War II afforded her the opportunity to learn from the ground floor about computers. Her training, native ability and perseverance very soon made her an authority on the emerging field of computers — a field to which she contributed for many years.

She was born in New York City on December 9, 1906, the first child of Mary Campbell (Van Horne) Murray and Walter Fletcher Murray. Another daughter and a son were born later. Walter was an insurance broker who at 11 had been brought to the United States from Scotland. As a girl, his wife showed an interest in mathematics. The daughter of a civil engineer, she sometimes accompanied her father when he was surveying in the city. Later a young Grace would do the same thing with her grandfather, and show her mother's interest in mathematics. A maternal great-grandfather had been a rear admiral in the United States Navy, foreshadowing Grace's future.

When the children were still young, their father had to have both legs amputated. He impressed his offspring with the belief that if he could walk with the aid of two wooden legs and canes, they could do anything. He held that boys and girls should have equal educational opportunities and that they should be able to support themselves. Grace remembered that when she was three, he pointed out Halley's Comet to her and believed that she would live to see it again in 1986.

She had memories of a happy childhood with summers spent on Lake Wentworth in Wolfeboro, New Hampshire; of educational toys and a dollhouse.

Reading books was a special pleasure and she enjoyed *St. Nicholas* magazine. Learning to play the piano, to knit, crochet and do needlework were part of her growing up. There was a family story that the oldest daughter disassembled alarm clocks to find out how they worked. Grace was educated at private schools. There was opportunity to participate in various sports, and this appealed to her. Every summer she was required to read 20 books and to write reports on them. At 16 she was sent to board at Hartridge School in Plainfield, New Jersey. Here she was encouraged to enter Vassar College in Poughkeepsie, New York. Opened in 1865, it was a leading institution of higher education for women.

Grace took the advice, enrolling as a freshman in 1924. The dean made it clear to entering students that study was the most important aspect of a student's life, reinforcing what Grace already knew. She intended to study math and physics, both subjects for which she had a bent. She soon found herself tutoring groups of students in the latter discipline. From the beginning, she related theoretical and practical aspects, and proved herself a good teacher. She managed to audit beginning courses in botany, physiology and geology as well as in business and economics, while she simultaneously pursued the regular course of study. She graduated in 1928 with a B.A. degree in mathematics and physics. Elected to Phi Beta Kappa honor society, she was also awarded a Vassar College Fellowship for advanced study elsewhere.

For two of her college years, Grace was joined by her sister Mary, also enrolled at Vassar. One of the highlights of Grace's college days was a ride in a barnstorming biplane with one engine and an open cockpit. This adventure cost her $10. Photographs taken at this period of her life show a small and attractive woman.

By 1930, she had received a master's degree in mathematics from Yale University. In June of that year, Grace married Vincent Foster Hopper, then an instructor in English at New York University. The couple had met in Wolfeboro a few years before. They spent their honeymoon in Europe, where Grace was fascinated by Stonehenge.

From 1931 until 1943, she was employed by Vassar as a member of its mathematics department, rising to the rank of associate professor. Yale awarded her the Ph.D. in 1934; the title of her dissertation was "The Irreducibility of Algebraic Equations." The Hoppers built a house in Poughkeepsie in 1939. It was designed to make it convenient for Grace's father to visit. Since it was difficult for him to climb stairs, there were a bedroom and bath on the first floor. Vincent's work kept him in New York City much of the time, but on weekends he took the train home to Poughkeepsie. In 1941, Grace attended New York University as Vassar Faculty Fellow.

With the entrance of the United States into World War II, Grace wanted to serve her country. After a brief stint of teaching at Barnard College in New York City, in 1943, she joined the WAVES (Women Accepted for Volunteer

**Grace Murray Hopper**
**(Courtesy Unisys Corporation)**

Emergency Service), a branch of the U.S. Naval Reserve. At that time, she was separated from her husband and would be divorced two years later. In 1944, Grace, at the age of 44, attended Midshipman's School and on graduation was commissioned lieutenant, junior grade. Her assignment was to the Bureau of Ordnance Computation at Harvard University. Here she began her long association with computers.

Charles Babbage (1792–1871), an English mathematician and inventor, designed a mechanical digital device capable of processing information as a modern computer does. Borrowing from Joseph Jacquard's idea of producing cloth patterns by loom, Babbage envisioned punched cards to govern the steps in a calculation. He did not, however, build the device he designed.

Mark I, the first information-processing digital computer, was not completed until 1944. It was designed by Howard Aiken, a Harvard professor, and built at the International Business Machines (IBM) laboratories at Endicott, New York. Located at Harvard, this huge electromechanical machine weighed 5 tons, was more than 50 feet in length, had more than 500 miles of wire and external controls that required manual settings. Bulky and cumbersome mechanical devices that often failed substituted for the vacuum tubes, transistors and microchips that would be used later in computers. The calculations it produced depended on holes punched on paper tape in set sequences. IBM electric typewriters could print out the results. Mark I's performance was looked on as miraculous — in one day, it made calculations that otherwise would have required six months.

When Hopper reported to the Bureau of Ordnance Computation Project, she met Aiken himself, then a commander in the naval reserve. Although he was a tough taskmaster, Hopper had respect and admiration for him, from whom she learned much. Besides Aiken and Hopper, two other officers and four enlisted men ran Mark I round the clock. This could necessitate staying all night on the scene; sometimes crew members were wakened from their sleep with an order to report there. With the press of war, the Navy required calculations pertaining to, for example, guns, rockets and mines; even wanted was information about the short waves that would follow the explosion of an atomic bomb.

Mark II, which succeeded Mark I, proved five times faster. Once when Mark II stopped suddenly, the cause of the trouble was found to be a moth in a relay. Hopper believed that the term debugging was based on its removal. The dead moth was put into a logbook, now in safekeeping at the Naval Museum at the Naval Surface Weapons Center in Dahlgren, Virginia. Mark III was next; with vacuum tubes and magnetic tapes, it was 50 times faster than Mark I. Mark IV, endorsed by the Air Force, was in service from 1952 to 1962. It was the last in the Harvard series of Automatic Sequence Controlled Calculators.

Hopper stayed at Harvard until 1949. Rather than return to Vassar, where she was offered a full professorship, she chose in 1946 to be a research fellow in engineering and applied physics at the Computation Laboratory, where work on the Marks was continuing. She mastered the operation of Mark II and III in addition to Mark I. Her training in mathematics and physics served her well. Equally important was her vision: She realized the potential of the computer.

WAVES younger than Grace could join the regular Navy. Her age precluded that, so she became part of the naval reserve. Although no longer on active duty, this afforded her opportunity to take courses of interest to her. Such courses are exemplified by solving the problem of fueling as fast as possible a task force at sea when the rates for pumping and receiving oil are known. Hopper loved the Navy, remaining a loyal and enthusiastic supporter all her life

The year 1949 saw her begin work as senior mathematician at Eckert-Mauchly Computer Corporation in Philadelphia. The company was just finishing the construction of BINAC (Binary Automatic Computer). It had been commissioned by Northrop Aircraft Corporation for the secret Snark Missile project, and Hopper was sent to Hawthorne, California, to teach employees at Northrop how to use it.

The next Eckert-Mauchly project was to design and build the first mass-produced electronic commercial computer — Universal Automatic Computer, UNIVAC I. Much smaller than Mark I, it measured 14½ feet in length and was one thousand times faster. It used magnetic tape for storing, processing and receiving information.

By 1952, Remington Rand had bought Eckert-Mauchly. (Three years later, Remington Rand was merged into Sperry Corporation, later known as UNISYS.)

The use of the binary code — in which digits are transmitted and recorded electronically by the pressure or absence of an electrical pulse or current — meant that programmers had to retype some commands for each new program. This was time-consuming and encouraged errors. Hopper advocated writing commands and placing them in shared libraries of code, to be called up for future use. (At Harvard she and her co-workers borrowed from one another filed pieces of code that had proven to be reliable.) She then succeeded in producing a program that translated symbolic mathematical code into machine language (0s and 1s) and allowed storage on magnetic tape for recall. This innovative idea led to her promotion to systems engineer, director of automatic programming development.

The development of computers progressed rapidly, and Hopper involved herself in it. As early as the 1952 presidential election, UNIVAC I correctly predicted an overwhelming victory for Dwight Eisenhower one hour after the polls closed and with 7 percent of the vote counted.

Always looking forward, Hopper realized that computers would be used more widely if nonmathematicians could program them; that the key to this was to write the program in English that would be translated into binary code. She used the letters of the alphabet as symbols for the computer to translate into binary code. This system came to be known as Flow-matic. It used such words as replace, move, and multiply to apply to data and to operation(s) required. Since most people still regarded computers as calculators, it was an uphill pull for her to promote her concept. But she did not give up, publishing her ideas and making them known through public presentations. When 1956 ended, UNIVAC I and II were using 20 statements in English.

Other computer languages were being developed elsewhere — for example, FORTRAN by IBM — and each language required a specific computer. In 1959, Hopper attended a meeting called to discuss the development of a common business language, a step essential to progress but difficult to implement. The following year, the Government Printing Office issued a report on COBOL (COmmon Business Oriented Language). Grace had served as technical advisor of the group that had produced COBOL, into which was incorporated Flowmatic. Since it could be used in different computers, it was independent of any specific computer manufacturer. Grace backed it for use at Sperry. An article in *The New York Times* of August 26, 1960, noted that "COBOL substituted simple English key words for present complicated numerical jargon understood only by electronic computer specialists to 'instruct' a computer in its function."

Hopper was winning her battle. By 1962, IBM had accepted COBOL language. The Department of Defense urged many businesses to adopt COBOL, and many complied in the interest of obtaining government contracts. COBOL was continuously updated and improved; in the 1990s, it is still used.

When she was 60, Hopper reluctantly retired from the naval reserve with the rank of commander. But within a few months, the Navy needed her to direct the standardization of computer programs and their languages for that service. She was given an office and a small staff in the Pentagon. Originally engaged for a eight-month stint, Hopper spent nearly 20 years as director of the Navy Programming Language Group in the Office of Information Systems Planning and Development. She was responsible for many publications such as the Navy manual, *Fundamentals of COBOL*. She attained the rank of commodore in 1983 and that of rear admiral in 1985. Her second and final retirement from the Navy was marked by a ceremony aboard the U.S.S. *Constitution*, "Old Ironsides," in 1986. At that time, she was awarded the Distinguished Service Medal.

That second retirement did not mean that Hopper stopped active work. She immediately became a senior consultant for Digital Equipment Corporation (DFC), remaining there until her death. She also traveled extensively to speak about computers and their future; she contributed her honoraria for these engagements to the Navy Relief Society.

Her second home was Wolfeboro, New Hampshire, where the Murrays had spent their summers and where her brother and his family resided. (By gubernatorial proclamation, November 7, 1983, was Captain Grace Murray Hopper Day throughout New Hampshire.)

"Amazing Grace," as she was called, received many honors, including some 40 honorary doctorates. Among other tributes, Data Processing Management Association named her "Man" of the Year in 1969; she was elected a Distinguished Fellow of the British Computer Society in 1973, the first American — male or female — to be so honored; in 1984, she was inducted into the Engineering and Science Hall of Fame; in 1991, President Bush presented her with the National Medal of Technology "for her pioneering accomplishments in the field of data processing." A naval vessel bears her name.

Grace Murray Hopper died the first day of 1992. She is buried at Arlington National Cemetery. She believed that young people must be given the best possible training. Her advice to them mirrored her own life's work: "A ship in port is safe, but that is not what ships are for. Be good ships. Sail out to sea and do new things."

# Chapter 17

# Rita Levi-Montalcini
## *Neurobiologist*

*I know enough of hate....* — Robert Frost

Anti-Semitism drove neurobiologist Rita Levi-Montalcini from her university laboratory to an improvised one in a bedroom of her home; it did not prevent her from winning a Nobel Prize.

Italy was a kingdom when Rita was born in Turin on April 22, 1909, to Adamo Levi and Adele Levi (Montalcini). Her siblings included an older brother as well as a non-identical twin named Paola. Rita, a rather timid child, was very close to her mother, while Paola favored her father. The children were brought up in a loving atmosphere in an educated family living in comfortable circumstances. From early childhood, the twins had an exceptionally close relationship with one another. Both parents were Jewish, Adele more tied to tradition than her husband. However, Rita was told by her father that she and her brother and sister were freethinkers; at 21, each could decide on a religious affiliation, if that was desired.

Adamo, an engineer by training, was a man of culture; three of his children would distinguish themselves: Gino, the son, as an architect; Rita as a scientist; Paola as a painter. (Daughter Nina married and had a family.) Late in life, Rita would write:

> The possible negative influence of having been born and raised in a Victorian climate, unsuited to my natural tendencies, was mitigated by my mother's complete acceptance of the role prescribed for women during the reign of Queen Victoria and the first two decades of this century. The absence of complexes, a remarkable tenacity in following the path I believe to be right, and a way of underestimating the obstacles between me and what I want to accomplish — a trait I believe I inherited from my father — have helped me enormously in facing the difficult years of life.

Rita's early education was in public school — her parents wanted her to know schoolmates from all social strata. Although she did well scholastically, her father decided she should enter middle school and then the girls' high school — a track that precluded entrance to a university. Adamo's thinking was influenced by the fact that two of his sisters — one with a doctoral degree in literature, the other in mathematics — had had great difficulty in reconciling their scholarly pursuits with marital and maternal obligations.

Rita had little interest in sports and had an early passion for trains. She showed little inclination to make friends with members of her own sex; her observance of the subordinate role of women in society had convinced her that she did not want to be a wife and mother. She believed that she had a bent for philosophy, but she needed a university education to pursue that. The result was that she felt somewhat isolated. Meanwhile she and Paola read such authors as the Swedish Selma Lagerlof and the British Brontë sisters.

In 1930, three years after she had left school, Rita decided to become a doctor. During World War l, she had had a childish desire to be a Red Cross nurse, believing that medicine was not open to her. The death of a loved governess from cancer of the stomach prompted her resolve to study medicine. Although her father did not approve, he made no attempt to stand in her way.

Her preparation for the university required tutors for the classics and mathematics. Her cousin Eugenia Lustig joined her, and the pair studied intensely for eight months, covering philosophy and history on their own. They successfully passed the required examinations.

Rita and Eugenia were among the seven girls in the freshman-sophomore class of about 300 at the University of Turin's medical school. After completing the first year with high honors, Rita became an intern at the Institute of Anatomy, headed by Giuseppe Levi, with whom she would have a long association. Levi assigned her to a tedious problem of counting nerve cells. This involved preparing mouse tissue for microscopic examination and then studying the sections made. Her next project entailed a study of the convolutions of the brains of human fetuses. The first difficulty here was the procurement of fetuses, especially since almost all abortions were clandestine. Liberated from that study, Rita's next assignment was the in-vitro culture of nervous tissue. The experience gained would be helpful in her future studies, and according to her, made her passionate about research.

A fellow-classmate of Rita's was Renato Dulbecco, a future Nobel Laureate. He became a fast friend of hers, but at a later period in her life. She remained rather aloof during her student days. She recalled, "the longed-for study of medicine seemed incompatible with the extracurricular activities preferred by the great majority of students in the 1930s." One male student who was seriously interested in her died at 28 of miliary tuberculosis. Her father

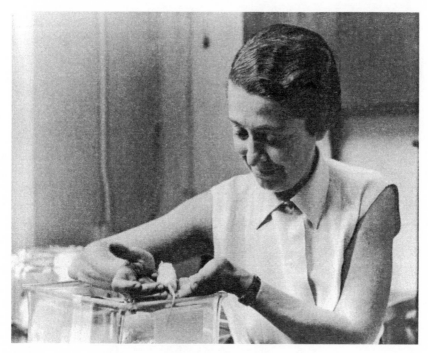

**Rita Levi-Montalcini**
**Circa 1959**
**(Courtesy University Archives, Washington University)**

also died while she was in medical school. His death was very traumatic to her, and her devotion to him increased posthumously. Perhaps this was because she had more or less feared him when he was alive. Rita (and Eugenia) graduated in 1936 with top honors.

An anti–Semitic campaign began in Italy in the spring of 1936. By January 1938, newspapers until then considered liberal had joined the chorus as the alliance with Nazi Germany drew closer. By November, marriage between "Aryan" and Jewish citizens was prohibited; Jews were suspended from all posts in the universities and academies. At the time, Levi-Montalcini was an assistant in Turin's Clinic for Nervous and Mental Diseases, where she was especially adept at microsurgery and silver staining. (Nerve cells require special staining with silver salts.) Her research covered the differentiation of nerve tissue in chick embryos in response to electrical stimuli. An Italian journal refused to publish her results because she was Jewish. (A Swiss journal accepted the paper later.) Regarding the existing atmosphere, Rita wrote:

> Among the regime's repressive maneuverings, the universal suspicion polluting all relationships, which is common to all totalitarian systems, was one

of the very worst.... In their natural wisdom the Italians found the anti-
Semitic campaign repugnant; and at the academic level, I remember not a
single manifestation of hostility toward me but only general demonstrations
of sympathy.... By March, 1939, I could no longer attend university insti-
tutes without risking denunciation or endangering Aryan friends.

Rita spent nine months in Brussels at a neurological institute. With the
outbreak of World War II and the likelihood that Hitler would invade Bel-
gium, she returned to Turin and her family. For a few months, she practiced
medicine under cover, treating poor patients who came to the medical clinic
at the university. Her activities were limited in that she needed the signature
of an Aryan doctor on a prescription. She finally ceased practice.

At the suggestion of Rodolfo Amprino, a friend from medical school
days, Rita in 1941 set up a makeshift laboratory in a bedroom of her home.
Necessary equipment for incubating embryos and for the preparation and
study of thin sections of tissue was accumulated with difficulty and required
some ingenuity. Her research was influenced by a 1934 article by Viktor Hamburger. Hamburger had shown that removal of the limb buds in a chick embryo
affected the nerve cells responsible for the innervation of the adult limbs. His
interpretation postulated an organizer that induced the differentiation of organs
and of whole embryos that come into direct contact with the tissue releasing
it; in the case of ablated limbs, there was a decrease of inductive factor.

Levi-Montalcini found that in embryos with excised limbs the differentiation of nerve cells proceeded normally, but that a degenerative process followed by nerve cell death began as soon as the fibers reached the stump of
the amputated limbs. This she believed was due to a factor whose role was
different from that envisioned by Hamburger. Investigation of many aspects
of this factor would occupy much of her professional life for years to come.

During the second half of 1942, the Allies' bombing of Turin became
severe. "Every time the alarm sounded," Rita wrote, "I would carry down to
the precarious safety of the cellars the Zeiss binocular microscope and my
most precious silver-stained embryonic sections." That fall, the family moved
to a small house in the hills, an hour away from Turin. The lab was moved
to an even smaller space than before.

Here is Rita's description of wintry days in her native city, now devas-
tated by night bombing raids: "The ruins of bombed buildings, broken pipe
lines, damaged electrical and telephone plants were swept aside and repaired
with unbelievable speed, but hopelessness and despair were written on everyone's face." The difficulty of obtaining fertilized eggs and the repeated power
failures that affected the incubator in which the embryos were developing did
not prevent her from finishing some important projects. The central theme
of these was the interaction of genetic and environmental factors in the regulation of the differentiation process of the nervous system during the early
stages of development.

On September 10, 1942, German tanks were seen in Turin. Rita and her family, fearing for their lives, boarded a train. Although thousands of Italians had offered Jews protection at grave risks to themselves, flight from the Nazis now seemed imperative. "Almost everyone ... was furnished with identity cards which had nothing in common with the real ones except sex and a plausible approximation to the right age," Rita wrote. They got off at Florence to avoid suspicion on the part of a Fascist officer whom Rita had known at the university. Rented a room by the family of a friend of Paola, she, Rita and their mother remained there for the duration of the war. It turned out later that their landlady, Consilia Leoncini, doubted that the Levi-Montalcinis were non–Jewish, as they claimed, but Consilia decided to play along with the deception. With the use of false names and ID cards created by Rita, her family survived. Although the cards showed serious discrepancies, which struck terror in the hearts of the bearers, these cards did not deter municipal officials from issuing life-sustaining ration cards.

By August, 1944 Florence was in a state of emergency as the Nazis made a last-ditch attempt to keep the city. They blew up bridges across the Arno River as part of the systematic destruction of ethnic and cultural values. This cut off food supplies; there was a shortage of water and electricity; scattered mines caused many deaths. According to Rita: "[The] mass movement of the population, before the final expulsion of the Germans and the arrival of the Allied armies, became the subject of one of Paola's most beautiful paintings of that period: 'The Walking City.'"

Giussepi Levi, Rita's medical school mentor, friend and advisor, had also fled to Florence. He was away in August, but when the emergency was declared, she managed to reach his apartment and rescue the manuscript of the revision of a massive textbook he had written.

On September 2, the British entered Florence. Rita wrote:

> For the first time I saw, after the soldiers had passed, a bus marked with a Star of David — now no longer an object of derision. Water tanks bearing the emblem were going around distributing water to the thirsty population. In a state of mind quite different from that in which we had presented our false IDs to receive our ration cards, we returned to the same offices to present our real ones — which we had kept jealously hidden during our clandestine life — to be recognized in our real identities.

Fighting continued in the Apennines between Italian partisans, British and Americans on one side, and Germans on the other. With a constantly shifting front, many families were moved by Allied trucks to live in temporary quarters. Rita went to work as a doctor-nurse for the Allies' health service, where she was located in a dilapidated military barracks. The refugee population included newborns — often extremely dehydrated — and babies and old people suffering from malnutrition and cold. Towards the end of winter, a serious typhoid fever epidemic broke out. Antibiotic treatment was not then available, so Rita saw many deaths. With regard to a specific patient, she wrote, "My sense of impotence in this case contributed to the decision I later took not to practice the profession. I lacked, in fact, the detachment that allows a doctor to face the suffering of a patient without creating an emotional involvement damaging to both parties."

With the German collapse in April, 1945, Mussolini was captured, tried in a summary court-martial and shot. Thus ended the Fascist regime.

Before returning to Turin, Rita and Gino located family members who had gone into hiding. Offered her previous position with Levi, Rita began neuroembryological research with Rudolfo Amprino. It was during this time that she struck up a friendship with Dulbecco.

Viktor Hamburger, whose work had spurred Levi-Montalcini to repeat and extend it, had read her conclusions, published in a Belgian journal. He wrote Levi that he hoped it could be arranged for Rita to visit his lab in Saint Louis for a semester.

In September, 1946, Levi-Montalcini sailed from Genoa for the United States. Aboard was Dulbecco, bound for Bloomington, Indiana, to work under Salvador Luria, who had been a class ahead of them at Turin, and a future Nobel Laureate. Dulbecco hoped to settle permanently in the States and move his wife and two children there. Rita knew that her mother and sister were too tied to Italy to move, so she was planning a short stay, as arranged. In reality, her stay lasted for 30 years, although she made frequent long visits to her native land. Living much of the time in Washington University housing, she became an American citizen in 1956, at the same time retaining her Italian citizenship.

That first year, she made friends with an Italian couple, Paulo and Silvia Rava, who adopted her. Sometimes on Sundays she had a sail on an old boat named *Admiral*; sometimes she went on departmental picnics to the Ozarks. She has been described as a short, slender women with gray-green eyes.

At times Levi-Montalcini had doubts about her future in neurobiology. During one of these periods, she went to Bloomington to consult with Luria, whose opinion she respected. By the fall of 1947, her doubts were laid to rest. She later explained, "The startling realization that nerve cell populations were subject to quotas, and to the elimination of excess numbers in their ranks, as well as to migrations that went hand in hand with functional differentiation showed that there were ontogenic [life cycle of a single organism] processes at work in the nervous system which were not as inaccessible to investigation as I had previously imagined."

Elmer Bueker at Georgetown University in Washington, D.C., had replaced one limb bud of a chicken embryo with a fragment of a bird or mammalian tumor. A mouse tumor, Sarcoma 180, grew vigorously and was invaded by nerve cells growing out from adjacent sensory ganglia (masses of nerve cells from which nerve impulses are transmitted). These were 33 percent larger than those innervating the normal limb bud on the opposite side of the embryo. On studying these results, Rita and Hamburger reasoned that the tumor was releasing some chemical factor that was in turn inducing remarkable growth of the sympathetic ganglia and exuberant branching of their nerve fibers. Rita postulated that if the tumors were releasing such chemical factors of hormonal nature, the effect would be apparent when an isolated sympathetic ganglion was incubated with the tumor in laboratory glassware.

Although Levi-Montalcini had had some experience with cell culture, the laboratory in Washington University did not provide this. She arranged to visit Rio De Janeiro, where a Turin friend, Hertha Meyer, had set up an in-vitro culture unit at the local Institute of Biophysics. At summer's end in 1952, Rita implanted some cells of Sarcoma 180 and of Sarcoma 37 into two little mice. She took them to Italy, where she visited her family, then boarded a plane for Brazil. The mice were confined in a small cardboard box and supplied with bits of apple.

Levi-Montalcini did not return to St. Louis for about five months. The work had its ups and downs, but she proved that the tumor tissue could exert its growth-enhancing effects on an isolated ganglion in tissue culture. It was a turning point in that only hours instead of weeks were needed to screen in cell culture potential sources of growth-promoting activity.

Deciding that she had earned some time off, Levi-Montalcini explored Rio and then visited Peru and Ecuador before flying to St. Louis in January 1953. Encouraged by Rita's progress in Rio, Hamburger hired a biochemist to purify what was now called Nerve Growth Factor (NGF). Selected to do the job was Stanley Cohen. Born in 1922 and the holder of a Ph.D. from the University of Michigan, he still limped from childhood polio. He and Rita collaborated on the NGF work until 1959, when Stan, as he was known, went to Vanderbilt University. It was found, fortuitously, that the factor was present in snake venom — more abundant and potent than that in tumor cells. Also, very potent NGF was isolated from mouse salivary glands. As other laboratories became interested in NGF, much information accumulated. It became evident that NGF was secreted by a variety of normal and malignant cells. A protein, its molecular weight, structure, and amino acid sequence were determined. By the 1980s, the DNA that codes for NGF and its originating gene had been discovered. When specific antibodies to NGF were made, they reduced the size of the sympathetic ganglia, with no ill effects on any other organs or tissues. For unexplained reasons, there was no damage to the peripherally located sympathetic ganglia that control the sex organs of both sexes. This made it possible to raise entire colonies of mice lacking in sympathetic nervous symptoms, but otherwise normal. Such animals have provided a valuable study model.

In 1961, Levi-Montalcini set up in Rome a small research unit that would collaborate with Washington University. The Italian Institute of Health provided workplace and equipment, and there was financial support from the National Research Council (Italy) and the National Science Foundation (U.S.). Rita and a colleague named Piero Angeletti alternately lived for six-month periods in Rome and St. Louis with NGF the object of their research, There was no problem of attracting able postdoctoral students to the project; it was, however, difficult to raise money for the operation. In 1969, it became an official organ of the National Research Council. Known as the Laboratory of Cell Biology, it included departments of neurobiology, cell biology, mechanisms of gene expression and immunology.

Today, NGF is produced in large quantities by genetic engineering. Rita herself asked, "Will the NGF derived from this new source ... be able to bring back order to the functionally impaired neuronal circuitries of that immensely complex entity, the brain of *Homo sapiens*?"

In 1977, Levi-Montalcini retired from her position at Washington University. She and Paola made their home in Rome, where they shared an apartment. Following her retirement as director of the Laboratory of Cell Biology in 1979, she was a guest researcher. Her autobiography, *In Praise of Imperfection,* came out in 1988. A fascinating work, translated from Italian, it takes its title from a poem by Yeats. Levi-Montalcini's *Your Life* was published in 1993.

She holds honorary degrees and is a member of such learned societies as Accademia Nazionale dei Lincei, the Pontifical Academy, the Accademia delle Scienze detta dei XL, the National Academy of Sciences and the Royal Society.

In 1986, at the age of 77, Rita Levi-Montalcini and Stanley Cohen shared the Nobel Prize in physiology or medicine for the discovery of NGF, a discovery that "opened new fields of widespread importance to basic science." The following year she went to the White House to receive the National Medal of Science from President Reagan.

In 1995, articles in a leading Swedish newspaper alleged that one of the members of the Nobel Committee had been closely related to Fidia, an Italian pharmaceutical company. The committee member was Thomas Hökfelt, a neurobiologist of international reputation. Fidia was accused of trying to influence Hökfelt to vote for Levi-Montalcini since her research was central to the interests of Fidia. Hökfelt had received the Fidia Research foundation's Golgi Award in 1986 and had been a member of one of Fidia's advisory boards. He claimed that his relationship with Fidia represented what was usual between researchers and industry.

An immediate inquiry was made by the Committee for Physiology or Medicine. Their report repudiated the suggestion that members had been unduly influenced; the Nobel award was made on the basis of the outstanding work of Levi-Montalcini.

Paola and Rita remain as close in old age as in early life. They believe in helping young people attain their career goals and both work toward that. Levi-Montalcini has served as president of the Italian Multiple Sclerosis Association.

Levi-Montalcini wrote in 1988:

I have become persuaded that, in scientific research, neither the degree of one's intelligence nor the ability to carry out one's tasks with thoroughness and precision are factors essential to personal success and fulfillment. Most important for the attaining of both ends are total dedication and a tendency to underestimate difficulties, which cause one to tackle problems that other more critical and acute persons instead opt to avoid.

# Chapter 18

# Rachel Carson
## *Ecologist and Writer*

*Only when man destroys the life and beauty of nature, there is outrage.* — George Macauley Trevelyn

Rachel Carson is considered one of the most important originators of the environmental movement. Her outstanding talent for writing made her message clear to the layman, but her credibility depended to a large degree on her scientific training.

Rachel Louise Carson was born in Springfield, Pennsylvania, on May 27, 1909. Of Scottish-Irish ancestry, she was the third child of Robert Warden Carson and Maria (McLean) Carson.

Robert Carson had signed a mortgage for a farm on a 64-acre parcel of rural land in Springdale, Pennsylvania. Later he tried to sell lots of this property at profit, but with little success. At various stages in his life, he sold insurance, real estate and products of his land; he worked as the operator of an electrical substation run by the local power company. Such efforts never brought him financial security, and his family had little money to spare.

Maria Carson's influence was intense and enduring. She was well educated, a reader and gifted musician. (She gave piano lessons to supplement the family income.) She had an intense love and understanding of nature, and this she imparted to her children.

Rachel's siblings were too old to be her close companions. She soon learned to be happy with her dogs, wild birds and such creatures rather than to seek the company of other children. She became a precocious reader and writer.

At age 10, she entered a contest for young writers sponsored by her favorite (and Grace Hopper's) *St. Nicholas Magazine.* Required was an article about fighter pilots. Rachel's brother, who was a member of the Army's air service in World War I, had written home about an experience in France of a Canadian fighter pilot who later instructed the brother. Rachel retold the story, winning a silver badge and publication of her work. This prompted her to write more stories before she reached her teens.

She graduated from Parnassus High School in 1925. Her aptitude for study had spurred her parents to send her to college despite their precarious financial situation. She had won $100 in the annual state scholarship examination and had unofficial financial aid from the college, but much more was needed to pay for tuition and board at Pennsylvania College for Women (later Chatham College). Meeting the expense was a constant struggle, with Rachel accumulating a debt to the institution. Maria sold china and silver to help.

Many of the students came from rich families and took part in the social life of the college. Rachel participated little in such activities, but she did make a few friends. She enjoyed the sports offered, field hockey in particular. Her mother visited almost weekly and showed an exaggerated interest in her daughter's progress. She helped by typing papers to save Rachel's time. (She would continue this practice with Rachel's manuscripts.) Maria's other children were having family problems, and perhaps she left home frequently to get away from the turmoil in her now crowded home. Rachel graduated magna cum laude in 1929.

Since she intended to be a professional writer, Rachel had chosen a major in English. As a science offering, she took introductory biology from Mary Scott Skinker, a professor known for high standards and rigorous requirements. Rachel found the subject fascinating and the instructor inspiring. Although she had won a prize for a short story, she decided to switch her major to biology, continuing, however, to work on the staff of the student newspaper. Her decision surprised some of the faculty; no one seemed to realize that a career combining biology and writing was possible.

Following the course pursued by Mary Skinker, who came to be Rachel's mentor, the recent graduate spent the first of many summers at Wood's Hole (see Chapter 1), aided by a scholarship. For years she had felt an attraction to the sea; now she could experience it.

In the fall, with scholarship aid, she entered Johns Hopkins University as a candidate for the master's degree. She graduated in 1932.

In 1930, Robert and Maria Carson had joined their daughter in Baltimore. The move was for economic reasons and at the same time, satisfied the unusual closeness between Rachel and Maria. In addition, Rachel did not care for homemaking, so her mother's presence gave her more time for other pursuits.

Lack of money continued to be a problem, especially because of the economic depression of the time. Attaining a Ph.D. was out of the question, so Rachel took whatever kind of work she could. For several years she held teaching or laboratory assistantships at Hopkins and for a short time at the

Rachel Carson
(Courtesy Curator of American Literature,
Beinecke Rare Book and Manuscript Li-
brary, Yale University)

University of Maryland. The death of her father in 1935 contributed to the family's dependence on Rachel.

It was a fortunate event when Elmer Higgins, head of the Division of Scientific Inquiry of the Bureau of Fisheries, hired Carson part-time to write radio scripts for a series entitled "Romance Under the Waters." Promotion to a full-time position as a government scientist soon followed. Her writing assignments required much library research.

Additional income was needed urgently after Rachel's sister died, leaving two young daughters for their aging and ailing grandmother to raise and their aunt to support. Rachel felt an urgency to earn more from commercial publications. She achieved success gradually. It was to her advantage that she was not shy in approaching editors about her ideas and that she was aggressive in her financial negotiations. As early as 1937, a communication from Edward Weeks, then acting editor of *Atlantic Monthly*, summed up Rachel's forte: "The findings of science you have illuminated in such a way as to fire the imagination of the layman."

Higgins had suggested that she send a particular essay to *Atlantic Monthly;* When she finally submitted "Undersea," it was accepted. It was so impressive that it led to a contract from Simon and Schuster to write *Under the Sea-Wind: A Naturalist's Picture of Ocean Life.* Published in 1941, this narrates the lives of creatures that inhabit the sea, which itself is the book's central character. Despite good reviews from scientists, sales were poor.

In 1940, the Bureaus of Fishery and Biological Survey merged to form the Fish and Wildlife Service of the Department of the Interior. Carson advanced in steps from assistant aquatic biologist (1942-43) to biologist and chief editor (1949-52). During World War II, one of her tasks was to promote little-known seafood sources of protein. Her training and standing in the department put her in a unique position of benefit to her off-the-job writing. She was in touch with ongoing research and authorities. She had above-average knowledge relating to the scientific and political problems in her field.

Officially and otherwise she managed to bird watch, take field trips, do tide-pool research in Maine and have all sorts of contacts with people as well as experiences that helped to shape her ideas on conservation and ecology. With regard to the latter, she had tried unsuccessfully in 1945 to persuade *Reader's Digest* that DDT (dichlorodiphenyltrichloroethane) was a dangerous pesticide.

In 1946, Carson rented a cabin on the Sheepscot River near Boothbay, Maine. Here she wandered on the beach, spending most of her time studying nature. She realized that she wanted to buy a place in the vicinity and then spend summers and as much more time as possible there. It would be seven years until she was able to build a cottage on Southport Island, Maine.

Because of her profound interest in ornithology, Carson was elected to the board of the District of Columbia Audubon Society in 1948. That same year, she noted: "The book I am writing is something I have had in mind a good while. I have had to wait to undertake it until at least part of the wartime oceanographic studies should be published, for I wanted to reflect some of the new concepts of the ocean that research has developed. Now there seems to be enough to go ahead on."

The book was *The Sea Around Us*. The necessary research involved consulting more than a thousand different sources, correspondence with oceanographers all over the world and personal discussions with experts. All this in addition to her government job and home responsibilities prompted Carson to find an agent to do her negotiating. She selected Marie Rodell, who represented her well and remained a good friend — a real asset to Rachel's career. In 1949, Rodell obtained a contract with Oxford University Press.

As author of a book about the sea, Carson wanted to have experienced underseas diving. She managed to do this in Florida, but only went to a depth of 15 feet. Also, she and her agent spent 10 days on a research vessel that was being used in a study of deep-sea commercial fishing around Georges Bank.

Worried that her book would be regarded as another "introduction to oceanography," Carson was particular about layout. Her own experience as an editor was valuable in such matters. The manuscript was delivered to the editor in July 1950 and published a year later. The *New Yorker* used an advance copy to run approximately half of the material as a three-part piece, "Profile of the Sea." A prepublication chapter in the *Yale Review*, "The Birth of an Island," won the George Westinghouse Science Writing Award of the American Association for the Advancement of Science.

Here is a sample of Carson's elegant prose:

> ...for the sea lies all about us. The commerce of all lands must cross it. The very winds that move over the lands have been cradled on its broad expanse and seek ever to return to it. The continents themselves dissolve and pass to the sea, in grain after grain of eroded land. So the rains that arose from it return again in rivers. In its mysterious past it encompasses all the dim origins

of life and receives in the end, after, it may be, many transmutations, the dead husks of that same life. For all at last return to the sea — to Oceanus, the ocean river, like the ever-flowing stream of time, the beginning and the end.

The book was a bestseller. Surprised that the author was a woman, people were curious about her, especially about her appearance. Cyrus Durgin of the *Boston Globe* wrote: "She is small and slender, with chestnut hair and eyes whose color has something of both the green and blue of sea water. She is trim and feminine, wears a soft pink nail polish and uses lipstick and powder expertly, but sparingly."

*The Sea Around Us* won the National Book Award for the best nonfiction book of 1951. On accepting the honor, Carson expressed a theme still associated with her name: "It is impossible to understand man without understanding his environment and the forces that have molded him physically and mentally." *The Sea* also won the John Burroughs Medal for a natural-history book of outstanding literary quality. Foreign translations were issued, as well as junior editions. Among other honors, the book brought its author four honorary degrees. RCA-Victor had her write album notes for Debussy's *Le Mer*, conducted by Arturo Toscanini. A documentary film based on her book was not to Rachel's liking, but it won an Academy Award.

To her liking, however, was the award of a Guggenheim Fellowship to write another book. Among other bonuses from the success of *The Sea* was the reissue by Oxford (Oxford had bought the rights from Simon and Schuster) of *Under the Sea-Wind*. This time it made the bestseller list. Royalties from the two books made it possible for Carson to resign in 1952 from her government position to devote herself to full-time writing.

Her neighbors at Southport Island were a couple named Dorothy and Stanley Freeman. The two women struck up a friendship that endured until Rachel died. When they parted at the end of each summer, they carried on a voluminous correspondence and sometimes found time to get together. During the period of their friendship, Rachel's life was particularly stressful. Her mother was becoming increasingly disabled and somewhat difficult. Marjorie, her niece, had a young child, and the three looked to Rachel for a home and support. Hiring a competent housekeeper, Ida Sprow, improved the situation. When Marjorie died in 1957, Rachel adopted her grandnephew Roger, then 5. Perhaps her closeness to Dorothy reflected her need to escape from her home responsibilities in a manner similar to her mother's.

*The Edge of the Sea* appeared in 1955. With black-and-white pencil drawings by Fish and Wildlife staff artist Bob Hines, it sold well and brought new honors. The citation of a 1956 award for the book noted: "Miss Carson has successfully invaded a man's field and with a poet's eye, a scientific mind, and a woman's intuition, has taught the world to wonder."

Her knowledge of biology led Carson to consider ominous any process that might upset nature's balance. She decided it was time to expose to her readers the havoc involved in the indiscriminate use of insecticides such as DOT, and to urge research into alternate methods to preserve crops. Although some other scientists had issued warnings, little attention had been accorded those warnings. Rachel would rely on her unique reputation both as a scientist and as a gifted writer to make her message believable.

Swiss chemist Paul Müller discovered in 1939 that DDT was an effective insecticide. Synthesized many years earlier, the compound was relatively inexpensive. It was effective in destroying lice, fleas and mosquitoes, which are vectors, respectively, of typhus and plague and of malaria and yellow fever. During and immediately following World War II, delousing with DDT had aborted serious outbreaks of typhus. This was in marked contrast to the situation in World War I, when more than 2 million lives were lost to that disease. DDT was responsible for a significant drop in the worldwide incidence of malaria. Müller won a 1948 Nobel Prize.

With the increased use of DDT, serious drawbacks became apparent: Many species of insects developed populations resistant to it; the compound, highly stable, accumulated in insects that were eaten by the animals, with the result that certain birds and fishes died; DDT proved to be carcinogenic.

Carson was fully aware that every statement she made would have to be backed up because vested interests such as the chemical and food-processing industries and government agencies such as the Department of Agriculture would fight her. Evaluation of the literature and consultation with experts proved to be very time-consuming. But she was resolved to do the job, saying that she could never again listen happily to a thrush sing if she had not done all she could.

There were distracting influences: *The Sea Around Us* needed revision for a new edition; Rachel was suffering with arthritis; her mother, to whom she was devoted and who had imbued in her a love of nature, died in 1958; most serious of all, in 1960, Rachel had surgery for cancer of the breast. The inexorable progression of the disease soon necessitated radiation therapy, cutting down on her productivity.

Previous to the issue of the book, a serialization began June 16, 1962, in the *New Yorker*. After the material for the book had gone to print, Velsicol Chemical Corporation of Chicago threatened suit, claiming there was in the serialization an inaccurate statement about the product Choldane. Houghton Mifflin, the publisher, refused to change the statement. No suit ensued.

*Silent Spring* was published in September 1962. The title refers to lines by Keats: "The sedge is wither'd from the lake / And no birds sing." The dedication was to Albert Schweitzer. The following excerpt demonstrates the clarity of Carson's explanations:

> One of the most sinister features of DDT and related chemicals is the way they are passed on from one organism to another through all the links of the

food chains. For example, fields of alfalfa are dusted with DDT; meal is later prepared from the alfalfa and fed to hens; the hens lay eggs which contain DDT. Or the hay, containing residues of 7 to 8 parts per million, may be fed to cows. The DDT will turn up in the milk in the amount of about 3 parts per million, but in butter made from this milk the concentration may run to 65 parts per million. Through such a process of transfer, what started out as a very small amount of DDT may end as a heavy concentration.

*Silent Spring* became another of Carson's bestsellers. One honor in which she took great pride was election to the American Academy of Arts and Letters. The citation read: "A scientist in the grand literary style of Galileo and Buffon, she has used her scientific insight and moral feeling to quicken our consciousness of living nature and alert us to the calamitous possibility that our shortsighted technological conquests might destroy the very source of our being."

There were also the criticisms she had anticipated; it was even claimed that because she lacked her doctorate, her credentials were weak. Unfortunately, she was too ill to enjoy some of the acclaim. Besides enduring great physical discomfort from advanced cancer and from arthritis and angina, she worried about Roger's future. It was ultimately worked out that Paul Brooks, Rachel's editor at Houghton Mifflin and a personal friend, would become the boy's guardian.

Rachel Louise Carson died in Silver Spring in 1964 at 56. Dorothy Freeman, in accord with Rachel's wishes, scattered some of her ashes along the rocky coast of the Sheepscot River in Maine. In 1965, thanks to the effort of Marie Rodell, Harper and Row published *The Sense of Wonder*. Involving children, this short book was dedicated to Roger.

In 1971, the Rachel Carson National Wildlife Refuge, which is located on the Maine coast, was dedicated. Nine years later, the Presidential Medal of Freedom was awarded posthumously to Carson, with Roger accepting it from President Carter. A Rachel Carson 17-cent postage stamp was issued in 1981. Her birthplace in Springdale has been restored and is open to the public.

Robert Downs included *Silent Spring* in his *Books That Changed America*, declaring it comparable in its impact on public consciousness and demand for instant action to Thomas Paine's *Common Sense*, to Harriet Beecher Stowe's *Uncle Tom's Cabin* and to Upton Sinclair's *The Jungle*. *Silent Spring* was also included in *The New York Public Library's Books of the Century*, published in 1996 by Oxford University Press.

As Carson had hoped, her book had a lasting effect on government policy. Following the publication of *Silent Spring*, President Kennedy appointed a special panel to study the effects of pesticides on the environment. The journal *Science* noted that this panel's report carefully balanced risks versus benefits and that it added up "to a fairly thorough-going vindication of Rachel Carson's *Silent Spring* thesis."

In 1970, the Environmental Protection Agency (EPA) was created by the government for "the protection, development and enhancement of the total environment." The Occupational Safety and Health Act (OSHA) was passed "to assure as far as possible every working man and woman in the Nation safe and healthful working conditions."

Carson knew that a book such as *Silent Spring* would require constant revision. With regard to her training at Hopkins, she noted, "This was the unforgettable lesson: We do not really know anything. What we think we know today is replaced by something else tomorrow." The statistics on this or that herbicide or pesticide will change. They do not constitute the central theme; they were facts used to reinforce her premise. The significance of *Silent Spring*, Carson's enduring monument, is that it forced ordinary people to think of the future in terms of the environment. It succeeded in doing this because the author was blessed with vision and an analytical mind. The continued problem of risk versus benefit is paramount but, thanks to Carson will receive more consideration.

An oil spill in California in 1969 prompted the organization of the first Earth Day, April 22, 1970. This gave great impetus to the environmental movement, which continues to grow. Terms seldom heard before *Silent Spring* are part of modern vocabulary: greenhouse effect, recycling, endangered species, food chain, toxic substances, wetlands, organic gardening and the like.

Carson's contribution is well expressed in the Presidential Medal of Freedom citation:

> Never silent in the face of destructive trends, Rachel Carson fed a spring of awareness across American and beyond. A biologist with a gentle, clear voice, she welcomed her audiences to her love of the sea, while with an equally clear determined voice she warned Americans of the dangers human beings themselves pose for their own environment. Always concerned, always eloquent, she created a tide of environmental consciousness that has not ebbed.

# Chapter 19

# Chien-Shiung Wu
## *Experimental Nuclear Physicist*

*"Obsessed with physics"*—Wolfgang Pauli about Chien-Shiung

Chien-Shiung played a prominent part in obtaining experimental proof of a theory that brought its originators the 1957 Nobel Prize in physics. In contrast to Maria Goeppart Mayer, who showed theoretically how facts fitted a hypothesis, Chien-Shiung and her collaborators obtained data that fitted a theory that until then was unproven and not believed.

She was born on May 31, 1912, in Liuhe, about 30 miles from Shanghai. Her father was Wu Zhongyi and her mother Fan Fuhua. The former had liberal ideas, formed by reading. An engineer, he had been part of the Chinese Revolution of 1911. On returning home, he opened a school for girls, reinforcing his belief in the emancipation of women. Fan Fuhua encouraged local families to educate their daughters; she also tried to end their practice of binding the feet of female children. Family life for Chien-Shiung was very pleasant, and she was raised in a nonrepressive atmosphere where books, magazines and newspapers were part of her family's life. She always remembered that her father's advice was to ignore the obstacles and keep walking forward.

At 9, Chien-Shiung had gone as far as possible in her father's school (later it was enlarged to include high school). Her family then sent her to a first-class boarding school where one of her father's friends was a teacher and where Western ideas were respected. She remained at Soochow Girls School from 1922 until she graduated with high honors in 1930. She had enrolled in the education division rather than the academic because there was no tuition and because positions were assured on completion of the course. However,

Chien-Shiung took advantage of the academic curriculum by studying borrowed mathematics, physics and chemistry texts far into the night. She termed this "self-learning." Self-learning convinced her that she wanted to learn more about physics. She also studied English, but she neither then or later really mastered the language. She became a leader of the high school's chapter of China's underground student movement, emulating her father.

Although she was accepted at the National Central University in Nanjing, Chien-Shiung believed herself poorly prepared in mathematics, chemistry and physics. With the encouragement of her father, she studied at home all summer. She enrolled as a mathematics student, but later transferred to physics, doing very well. She graduated in 1936. Years later, she gave her father credit for the fact that she was a famous physicist in the United States, rather than a grade school teacher in China.

She taught at a provincial university during the year following her graduation. The next year, she did research in X-ray crystallography at the National Academy of Sciences in Shanghai. At the urging of a woman scientist there, she began to look to the United States for graduate work since her own country did not offer what she wanted. Fortunately help came from an uncle who was very fond of her. He had become financially successful by starting China's first long-distance bus company, and he offered to help pay her way to the United States.

Chien-Shiung had originally planned to study at the University of Michigan, where there were hundreds of Chinese students. Instead, she entered the University of California at Berkeley in 1936, attracted to its physics department by such scientists as Ernest Lawrence and Robert Oppenheimer. Lawrence had invented the cyclotron, or particle accelerator, that produced artificially radioactive elements and neutrons useful in nuclear, chemical and biological research. Oppenheimer, of atom bomb fame, was teaching quantum mechanics there.

At Berkeley Chien-Shiung met her future husband, Yuan Chiu-liu (Luke Yuan, according to his own Americanization of his name) who was also a Chinese graduate student in physics. She became acquainted with Ursula Schaefer, a student from Germany, at International House, her dormitory that housed foreign and American graduate students. The girls got along well, each intent on absorbing the other's culture. Their friendship would continue for many years. Chien-Shiung did not care for American food, and solved the problem by buying cheap leftovers from a Chinese caterer. Ursula liked Chinese food, too, and she, Chien-Shiung and Yuan often ate together. Chien-Shiung was popular in Berkeley and noted for her beauty and her smile. She seldom dressed in Western style; Chinese dresses with high collars and slit skirts suited her fine figure, and she ordered them from China and Taiwan.

She fared well professionally, too. Emilio Segrè, who later shared the 1959 Nobel Prize for physics, was a faculty member who became her friend; he

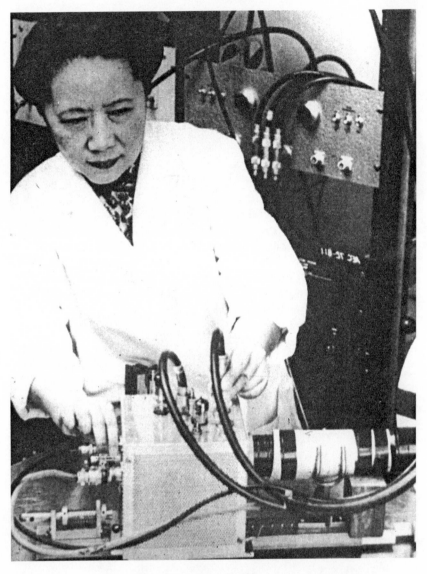

**Chien-Shiung Wu**
**(Courtesy AIP Emilio Segrè Visual Archives)**

noted that her will power and devotion to work were reminiscent of Marie Curie, but that she, Chien-Shiung, was more worldly, elegant and witty. The department recommended her for a fellowship to be held during her second year, but the university's administration did not approve it. Working extremely hard, she received the Ph.D. in nuclear physics in 1940.

When the Japanese invaded China in 1937, Chien-Shiung was cut off from all communication with her family. (She did not hear from them until the end of World War II.) However, she was very soon assured by her department head that she would be taken care of. She even received the sympathy of two young Japanese students who resided at International House.

Chien-Shiung spent the two years following graduation as a research assistant at Berkeley. She had become an expert on nuclear fission, lecturing nationally in 1941. Segrè faulted the University of California at Berkeley for failing to hire her on a permanent basis, claiming, "They would have had a star."

On the personal side, she was as attractive as ever: a newspaper reporter described her as looking "as though she might be an actress or an artist or a daughter of wealth in search of Occidental culture."

In 1942, she married Yuan at the home of Robert Millikan. Yuan had moved from Berkeley to California Institute of Technology in Pasadena to work under Millikan, winner of the 1923 Nobel Prize for physics.

Berkeley was less attractive to Chien-Shiung than it had been, mainly because some of its stars were engaged elsewhere in war research. When Yuan was hired by Radio Corporation of America laboratories in Princeton, New Jersey, to design radar devices, Chien-Shiung taught at Smith College in Northampton, Massachusetts. They met on weekends in New York City.

As an assistant professor at Smith, Chien-Shiung's primary duty was teaching. Obviously, this left little time for research, had adequate research facilities been available. Through Millikan she was offered several more attractive positions. She chose to work at Princeton University since her husband was working in that locality. She taught physics to engineering students who were receiving accelerated training because of the press of war.

Her career at Princeton was short lived. In March 1944, she joined the Manhattan Project at Columbia University to develop instruments to detect radiation.

After the war, she remained at Columbia, pursuing the subject of beta-decay, an area in which she had had previous experience. Beta-decay refers to a type of radiation produced when an atom disintegrates either naturally or artificially (by cyclotron or nuclear reactor). In either case, nuclear particles, anti-particles and new atoms may be produced. Chien-Shiung concentrated on trying to prove experimentally that Fermi's prediction about the speed of the electrons involved in beta-decay was correct. At the time, results obtained by others did not agree with Fermi's theory. Chien-Shiung eventually devised methods that proved Fermi correct.

In 1945, there was welcome news that her family was well. When both she and Yuan were offered professorships at the National Central University in China, Wu Zhongri advised his daughter against their returning to the land of their birth. This was because they would be refused reentry visas to the United States. Yuan and Chien-Shiung obtained United States citizenship in 1954.

In 1947, they had a son, Vincent Weichen Yuan, who would become a physicist. His parents moved to an apartment two blocks from Chien-Shiung's lab. Later on, she listed three musts for a married woman to be a success in science: a nice husband, a home close to work and good child care. Entirely engrossed in her work, working long hours in the laboratory and taking short periods for meals, she expected the same of her students.

Yuan made a name for himself by designing accelerators at Brookhaven National Laboratory. His technical expertise was most useful to his wife and her students. Since Brookhaven was too far from New York City for him to commute, he was home only on weekends. During his elementary school days, Vincent was sent to a boarding school near Brookhaven; this meant that he could return to New York with his father on weekends.

After Chien-Shiung accepted teaching responsibilities, she became an associate professor with tenure. In 1956 she was approached by Tsung-Dao Lee from Columbia and Chen Ning Yang of the Institute for Advanced Study at Princeton. These theoretical physicists were refuting the law of parity, for 30 years considered basic to the understanding of atomic disintegration. It stated that at the subatomic level, nature does not distinguish between left- and right-handed configuration; if a nuclear reaction or decay occurs in nature, so does its mirror image and with equal frequency. Lee and Yang could find no experimental evidence that this hypothesis was valid, and they wrote an article that suggested some experiments to settle the question. (They recognized that parity held for all strong and electro-magnetic interactions.)

One of their ideas was to measure the electron emission in beta-decay from oriented nuclei to see if the intensity changed when the polarizing field was reversed. Forward-backward asymmetry would disprove parity.

Chien-Shiung and Yuan were planning a trip to Europe to celebrate the anniversary of their arrival in the United States 20 years earlier. They intended to sail on the *Queen Elizabeth*, attend a physics conference in Geneva and conduct a lecture tour in the Far East. As it turned out, Yuan went alone; his wife could not bear the thought that someone else might launch a crucial experiment to disprove parity before she did.

The National Bureau of Standards in Washington, D.C., had facilities to cool materials close to absolute zero — and this condition was necessary for the experiment Chien-Shiung was about to conduct. In late July 1956, Ernest Ambler and three colleagues at the Bureau agreed to collaborate with Chien-Shiung in carrying out the experiment. Since she was based in New York, she visited Washington frequently to be sure that every detail was carried out as planned. By December, the experiments showed clearly that parity is not conserved in beta-decay. The details were published in *Physical Review* . Wu was listed as first author, with Ambler and the rest of the Bureau workers on a separate line.

The work was often referred to as the "Wu experiment," and made Chien-Shiung world-famous. Lee and Yang won the 1957 Nobel Prize for physics; she was not a recipient. However, over a period of time, numerous honors were bestowed on her: election to the National Academy of Science, many honorary degrees, the National Medal of Science from President Ford, and so on. An asteroid is named for Chien-Shiung Wu.

John McClaughry was a student in 1960 in her Advanced Nuclear Physics. He was impressed with her power of concentration under less than favorable circumstances:

> ...there was heavy construction going on outside, with lots of cement trucks backing and pouring.
>
> Prof. Wu was a tiny birdlike woman. She typically roamed back and forth, only the top third of her visible, behind the lab desk. Her English was still heavily accented, and her voice was soft. This made comprehension difficult.
>
> On a day I remember vividly, the cement trucks were in full voice outside the classroom. Prof. Wu announced that she would present the equation for some nuclear event or other. Then she turned to the blackboard, facing away from the class. and began to put terms on the board. As she added terms — eventually seven or eight, which covered at least 15 feet of blackboard — she endeavored to explain why they were being added. Unfortunately it was hard to see the terms from halfway back in the room, and almost impossible to hear what she was saying.
>
> Finally she turned triumphantly to the class, smiled, and said something like, "Now there — that's the complete description of...." The bell rang, and she departed. I was left staring at this enormously long equation about which I understood virtually nothing, although I am sure she explained every term to the blackboard as she was adding them.
>
> Lee and Yang had won the Nobel Prize 3 years earlier, and there was some sentiment that Mme. Wu should have shared it, for doing this incredibly difficult experiment at absolute vacuum near absolute zero.

In 1963, she did an experiment that confirmed a hypothesis proposed by Richard Feynman and Murray Gell-Man of Caltech. Previous experiments by others had not. Two years later, Chien-Shiung wrote *Beta Decay*, which became a standard reference book for physicists,

Over the years, as Communist control of China grew, Chien-Shiung had less and less contact with her family. When she finally got back to China in 1973, her parents and brothers were dead.

Before her retirement in 1981, she studied sickle cell anemia — an entirely different sort of problem. Following retirement, she traveled to China and Taiwan to lecture and advise scientists. She also encouraged women to become scientists, believing that the chief bar to their progress in this direction is "unimpeachable tradition."

She died on February 16, 1997, at the age of 84.

On the 40th anniversary of the famous paper by Wu, et al. and close to the time of her death, an interesting article by two physicists, Kurti and Sutton, appeared in *Nature*. It stressed that the parity violation experiment was a collaborative team effort, but that Chien-Shiung's name was listed first because the chivalrous suggestion was made that as the only woman, she might sign first.

Whether or not she deserved the accolades she received on the basis of the *Physical Review* article, cannot be known. That aside, Chien-Shiung was certainly one of the world's outstanding physicists. Her message to young scientists remains: "It is the courage to doubt what has long been established, the incessant search for its verification and proof that pushed the wheel of science forward."

# Chapter 20

# Ruth Sager
## *Geneticist*

*I would rather be right than be President.* — Henry Clay

Ruth Sager described a mode of inheritance additional to and not in accord with the classical genetics of Mendel. Like Barbara McClintock, she had faith in her findings, and ultimately succeeded in convincing her colleagues.

Sager was born on February 7, 1918, in Chicago to advertising executive Leon B. Sager and Deborah (Borovik) Sager. Ruth and her two sisters were brought up in an atmosphere of culture where learning was respected and encouraged. At 16, she graduated from New Trier High School in Winnetka, Illinois.

A favorite uncle urged her to go to "the best possible school," which, according to his thinking, was the University of Chicago. Although she entered "totally uninterested in science," she pursued a premedical curriculum. Later she decided on a career in research, graduating Phi Beta Kappa in 1938 with a B.S. degree in physiology.

After a period when she did secretarial work, Ruth enrolled as a graduate student in the plant physiology program at Rutgers University, from which she earned the M.S. in 1944. That same year, she married Seymour Melman. The marriage ended in divorce.

In 1945, Sager became a doctoral candidate at Columbia University. She worked under botanist Marcus Rhoades on corn genetics, the field of investigation that had intrigued Barbara McClintock. Sager referred to genetics as "the core science of biology." She obtained her Ph.D. in 1948. She was described at the time as having a pleasing personality.

The young geneticist spent that summer at the Hopkins Marine Station in Pacific Grove, California, preparing herself for a new problem — a problem

119

that would occupy much of her professional life. (Nettie Stevens had been at Pacific Grove for four seasons.) Working from 1948 to 1951 under a Merck postdoctoral fellowship from the National Research Council, Sager was employed at the then Rockefeller Institute for Medical Research in the laboratory of Sam Granick. Her project was to investigate the chloroplast, the cell's organelle that carries on photosynthesis. With advice from Gilbert Morgan Smith, she selected for her test organism the green alga *Chlamydomonas reinhardi*. Its chloroplast was large; the organism could be grown on laboratory media and subjected to the techniques of microbiology. Of great importance, it lent itself to genetic analysis — normally asexual, this alga is capable also of sexual reproduction. Sager continued at Rockefeller until 1955 as a staff member. It was during this period that she began work leading to the discovery that brought her fame.

It had been suggested as early as 1909 that the cell had genetic material other than the genes of the chromosome. However, classical genetics assumed no extranuclear genetic material. Sager began to believe there was validity in the former idea.

In 1955, she moved to Columbia University, where for the next 11 years, she held positions in the zoology department. By 1961, Sager and Yoshihiro Tsubo had devised ways to produce mutant strains of *Chlamydonas reinhardi*. Some of the mutants could not produce carbohydrate from carbon dioxide and water; some were temperature sensitive; some were resistant to the antibiotic streptomycin, and so on. By appropriate crossing, it was demonstrated that the rules of Mendelian inheritance did not apply. In other words, the evidence indicated that the cell supported, in addition to the usual type, an extrachromosomal type of inheritance that operated in the cytoplasm. Experiments with the streptomycin-resistant mutant showed that the resistance was inherited through the maternal side, not through both parents, as Mendelian inheritance requires.

By 1963, Sager and M. Ishida had isolated chloroplasts and proved they contained DNA, the hereditary material of the cell. The new findings offered an unproven concept involving the evolution of organisms — that chloroplasts and mitochondria, their counterparts in animal cells, represent an earlier system for reproduction.

In 1961, *Cell Heredity*, a text by Ruth Sager and Francis Ryan, combined modern genetics and the classical approach. The publisher was Wiley.

In 1962, Sager spent a year at the University of Edinburgh. Four years later, she was appointed professor of biology at Hunter College, where she remained until 1975. Continuing research that bolstered her position on extranuclear inheritance, she was the first to publish extensive mapping data on the genetic system of an organelle.

Her second book, *Cytoplasmic Genes and Organelles*, was published in 1972 by Academic Press. Much of it was written during summers spent at Woods Hole Marine Biological Laboratory.

In an interview by Andrew Campbell in 1994, Sager noted the opposition to her new scientific concept, remarking, "I don't think I ever gave an invited talk on the whole subject until I became a member of the National Academy [of Sciences], in 1977."

Out of curiosity, this writer consulted the widely used text, *Biological Science*, by William T. Keeton. The copyright date was 1967. There is very brief reference, without attribution, to cytoplasmic inheritance. *Cell Heredity* is cited under "References," as is Sager's January 1965 *Scientific American* article, under "Suggested Readings."

**Ruth Sager**
**(Courtesy Arthur Pardee)**

In the 1970s, Sager's research changed its focus to investigate the molecular basis of cancer of the breast. She spent 1972-73 at the Imperial Cancer Research Fund Laboratory in London. She was encouraged in this new approach by cancer researcher Arthur Pardee, whom she would marry in 1973.

From 1975 until her death in 1997, Sager was chief of the Division of Cancer Genetics at the Dana-Farber Cancer Institute in Boston. She was also professor of cellular genetics in the Department of Microbiology and Molecular Genetics at Harvard Medical School from 1975 to 1988. Arthur Pardee, who held joint appointments at Dana-Farber and Harvard Medical School, was supportive of his wife's work, and the union was a happy one.

Working with human cells, Sager identified genes that are underexpressed in cancer as compared to normal tissue. Such genes are termed "suppressor," and she was one of the first to promote their importance. (At the time, there was more interest in mutant genes as a cause of cancer.) She was especially interested in a gene that produced a growth-inhibiting protein called maspin (*ma*mmary *s*erine *p*rotease *in*hibitor). Sager found that normal breast cells contained maspin; tumor cells that had not metastasized contained very little, while cells that had spread to lung or lymph node contained none. She envisioned the ultimate use of therapeutic drugs to reactivate tumor-suppressior genes, or of gene therapy, using the tumor-suppressor DNA itself.

Just a short time before her death, the *Proceedings of the National Academy of Sciences* published a paper in which Sager reported success in isolating more than 100 candidate tumor suppressor genes from human tissue. Time will judge the significance of suppressor genes.

Their isolation has been accomplished by a procedure called differential display (DD), invented by Arthur Pardee. The latter described it as a way to find which genes are active — identified by their making messenger RNA in a given cell .

Several honors came to Sager late in her career. She was one of 21 researchers who received an Outstanding Investigator Award from the National Cancer Institute in 1985. In 1988, she was awarded the Gilbert Smith Medal from the National Academy of Sciences. Sager was chosen as the Princess Takamatso Lecturer in Japan in 1990. Four years later, her alma mater, the University of Chicago, made her Alumna of the Year.

Described as a tall, striking brunette with a ready smile, she once depicted herself as "probably the happiest person I know." She collected modern art and considered it the subject she knew "second most about."

Ruth Sager died in Brookline, Massachusetts, on March 29, 1997, from cancer of the bladder.

Following her death, a news release from Dana-Farber noted: "For more than half a century Ruth Sager has been a role model for women in health-related scientific research.... she demonstrated vision, insight and determination to develop novel scientific concepts in the face of established dogmas.... Her pioneering researches and original ideas continue to make contributions to biology."

# Chapter 21

# Gertrude Elion
## *Therapeutic Drug Designer*

*Work is love made visible.* — Kahlil Gibran

Gertrude Belle Elion did not have an earned doctorate, but her accomplishments brought her some 20 honorary doctorates and a Nobel Prize. Her life's work involved the production of several very important drugs.

Known as Trudy, she was born in New York City on January 23, 1918, the daughter of Robert and Bertha (Cohen) Elion. The parents were immigrants, Robert from Lithuania and Bertha from Russia. Both were Jewish and came from scholarly families. An immigrant grandfather spoke Yiddish with her and had an important influence on her life. All three of these close relatives respected education and encouraged her in that line. Bertha made it clear that a woman should be financially independent of her husband and believed that education was the key to that status.

When Trudy's brother Herbert was born, the family moved to the Bronx, then more rural than it is now. Robert Elion had worked his way through dental school and was doing well financially until the stock market crash of 1929, which left him bankrupt, for he had invested heavily.

His red-haired daughter was studious and wanted to obtain knowledge in many fields. She later recalled being very impressed by Paul de Kruif's 1926 book, *Microbe Hunters.* Her father loved opera, and at an early age she was taken to performances of the Metropolitan Opera Association. Music became part of her life, and as an adult, she continued to attend the Met, despite the distances sometimes involved to go to New York. After graduation from high school, Trudy entered Hunter College, the women's section of City College of New York. Tuition was free, but acceptance was competitive, with the result that all the students were of high academic caliber. Since Trudy's goal was to engage in some sort of cancer research, she chose chemistry

**Gertrude Elion**
**(Courtesy Glaxo Wellcome Heritage Center)**

as her major. In 1937, she graduated from Hunter with highest honors, a Phi Beta Kappa.

She needed financial assistance to pursue an advanced degree. She applied to 15 graduate schools, but was offered nothing. During the Depression years, little monetary aid was available, and there was a general feeling in academic circles that the support of men rather than women was economically more effective.

For several years, Elion, as had countless other qualified persons, took whatever kind of a job she could find. Among other endeavors, she taught nursing students as well as high school students; she did analytical quality control work for Quaker Maid Company; she worked in organic synthesis at Johnson & Johnson. Although this was not what she wanted, the experiences proved of some benefit, such as making her familiar with certain types of instrumentation. She was also gaining credits towards a master's degree, which she obtained from New York University in 1941.

As the United States became more and more involved in World War II, men were drawn into war-related industries and the military, leaving positions open to women. In 1926, when she was 26, Elion found the kind of position she desired at Burroughs Wellcome. She remained there throughout her professional life.

Trudy had approached the company at the suggestion of her father, who was familiar with Burroughs and Wellcome's Empirin from his dental practice. At the time, the business was run to benefit the Wellcome Trust, which supported research laboratories. Founded in England in 1880 by American pharmacists Silas Burroughs and Henry Wellcome, the company's mission was to research drugs that would treat serious diseases. Wellcome assured scientists that if they had ideas, they would be free to develop them. An American subsidiary of Burroughs Wellcome was then located in the New York suburb of Tuchahoe.

Trudy was hired by George Hitchings. On looking at her record and on the strength of an interview, he was convinced that she was worth the $50 per week she was asking. Hitchings was then working on the chemistry of two cellular constituents: DNA (deoxyribose nucleic acid) and RNA (ribose nucleic acid). By 1942 it was known that DNA transmitted genetic information, but how this took place was not understood. Hitchings was seeking ways to interfere with the production of the large amounts of nucleic acid involved in the reproduction of tumor cells. He preferred an approach based on reasonable theory rather than on trial and error. His idea was to use competitive inhibition to block tumor growth. This phenomenon is possible when substances that enter into complex formation with an enzyme are not absolutely specific for that enzyme; for example, if an essential component of nucleic acid is replaced by a similar component, known as an analog, tumor growth can be blocked. (In other words: the analog is a disguise to fool a cancer cell.)

Hitchings assigned Elion the study of purines, a group of essential components of DNA. By 1950, she had found that an analog named 2,8-diaminopurine showed promise in laboratory tests. After animal tests were made at Sloan Kettering Memorial Hospital in New York, it was given to two patients diagnosed with acute lymphatic leukemia. One had a two-year remission — a great encouragement to Elion and Hitchings because, without treatment, 95 percent of patients with the disease were dead within a year.

Elion was working extremely hard. However, she loved her job and voluntarily expended time and effort on it . Her fiancé had died some years before, and she seemed content to make work the focus of her life. For two years she studied towards a Ph.D. at Brooklyn Polytechnic Institute. When she reached a point where she was required to become a full time student, she reluctantly gave up. Hitchings gave her promotions and allowed her to publish her findings as first author. After some 20 of her papers had reached publication, he saw that she was elected to the American Society of Biological Chemists.

The success of 2,8-diaminopurine spurred her to look for a less toxic analog. She synthesized 6-mercaptopurine by substituting a sulfur for an oxygen atom on a purine molecule. Released for commercial use in 1953, it proved very effective, though not a cure, when used in conjunction with other drugs. Four months after release, the New York Academy of Sciences sponsored a symposium on its use. Elion continued the work, studying how 6-MP was metabolized in the body; her hope was to prevent the relapses that commonly occurred.

Many years later, Hitchings explained why there were relapses. He referred to "the horrible protocols that we dealt with," adding, "It was not entirely the clinicians' fault that multiple drugs were used in sequence. It was partly our fault because we could not give them enough of a drug to do a whole initial study with one drug." Elion also synthesized thioguanine, a purine analog to be used in conjunction with antileukemic drugs.

Another chapter was added to the 6-MP story. At the New England Medical Center in Boston, Robert Schwartz and William Dameshek had been unsuccessful in transplanting bone marrow. Then they found that 6-MP would suppress the host's immune response. After reading about this, Roy Calne of St. Mary's Hospital in London successfully used 6-MP to extend the life of a transplanted kidney in a dog. Calne won a Commonwealth Fund Fellowship to work at Peter Bent Brigham Hospital in Boston, the hospital where James Murray was endeavoring, with little success, to transplant kidneys across a genetic barrier (donor and recipient were not identical twins). When Calne visited Tuckahoe, he was given some samples to try. One of these, a derivative of 6-MP, kept alive a collie named Lollipop for 230 days after she received a transplanted kidney. When she died, her death was unrelated to rejection or the effect of Imurin, the drug used. Imurin proved to be very effective in human transplantation, making the procedure much more common. This immunosuppressive drug was first used in 1967 for a heart transplant patient. It is also given in certain autoimmune diseases.

Allopurinol is another drug that resulted from Elion's investigations. Clinical trials began in 1963. An analog of a purine named hypoxanthine, it is given to treat hyperuricemia, or the accumulation of excessive amounts of uric acid in the blood. This condition may be primary, as in gout, or secondary to certain diseases such as the leukemias. It may also occur where there is renal damage and when there is rapid tissue destruction due to radiation or chemotherapy. The end results are often kidney stones or painful deposits of uric acid crystals in the joints.

After 23 years of collaboration with Elion, Hitchings became vice president of research at Burroughs Wellcome in 1962. Trudy was then on her own as head of the department of experimental therapy.

On learning that a compound similar to her diaminopurine had some antiviral activity, she began work in that field. The effort would continue for four years. Chemotherapy of viral infections is different from that of microbial infections. This is because a virus replicates in a host cell, taking control of its mechanism for nucleic acid and protein synthesis. Interference with viral replication is likely to interfere with normal cell reproduction also. *A Short Textbook of Medical Microbiology*, published in 1973, has this statement: "Much hard work has gone into the search for anti virus agents, but so far it has had little success." Burroughs Wellcome's great success was acyclovir, an analog related to the purine guanine. It has proved effective against human herpes viruses (herpes infections may become life-threatening when the immune system is compromised), varicella-zoster virus (chicken pox and shingles), Epstein-Barr virus and cytomegalovirus. The discovery of acyclovir was announced publicly in 1974. Marketed as Zovirax, it brought millions of dollars in sales.

Burroughs Wellcome moved to Research Triangle Park, North Carolina, in 1970. It took Elion a little time to adapt to the rural atmosphere. With a newfound friend, she became a world traveler. Eventually she became enthusiastic about her new location.

After she retired in 1983, the group that she had led produced AZT, the drug used to treat AIDS. She claims none of the credit, other than that she trained them in the methodology.

In 1988, Hitchings, then 83, and Elion, then 70, shared the Nobel Prize for physiology or medicine with Scottish pharmacologist James W. Black, who had made many contributions to the area of drug treatment. According to the Nobel Committee: "While drug development had earlier mainly been built on chemical modification of natural products, [Hitchings and Elion] introduced a more rational approach based on the understanding of basic biochemical and physiological processes."

Both laureates made it clear that great as the honor was, their real satisfaction was from the knowledge that their work had saved lives. When she went to Stockholm, Trudy invited her niece and three nephews plus their spouses and children to attend the festivities.

She received many other honors, including the National Medal of Science from President Bush. When Burroughs Wellcome gave her $250,000 to donate to charity, she presented it to Hunter College for women's fellowships in chemistry and biochemistry.

Today, the Gertrude B. Elion Cancer Research Award provided by Glaxo Wellcome Oncology recognizes research excellence in cancer etiology, diagnosis, treatment or prevention by annually providing $30,000 to a promising scientist.

Known for her social conscience, Elion has continued altruistic pursuits. In 1998, she noted the things she does in "retirement":

- Serves as full-time consultant at Glaxo Wellcome.
- Mentors a third year medical student in research at Duke University.
- Serves on the following boards: Directors — Burroughs Wellcome Fund; Directors — Kenan Institute of Science Engineering and Technology; Overseers — Brown University School of Medicine; and Trustees — North Carolina High School of Science and Mathematics.
- Gives lectures at universities, medical schools, pharmacy schools and veterinary schools on her work.

Gertrude Elion's career should inspire women of ability who are willing to work hard in science; she lacked the customary doctorate, but she had brains and the stamina to persevere.

# Chapter 22

# Rosalyn Yalow
## *Medical Physicist*

*There are science and the application of science, bound
together as the fruit to the tree which bears it.* — Louis Pasteur

Rosalyn Yalow, as did Gerty Cori and Gertrude Elion, collaborated with
another scientist to do research that won a Nobel Prize. She worked under
the Veterans Administration, not in the more usual academic situation.

She was born on July 19, 1920, in New York City's Lower East Side, the
second child of Simon and Clara (Zipper) Sussman. Her parents were Jewish: Simon was an American-born son of Russian immigrants, while Clara
was brought from Germany as a young child. Both had little formal education, but both held learning in high regard. This attribute later manifested
itself in their son and daughter. Simon had a small paper and twine business,
and his wife did garment piecework at home. As a member of a family with
limited means and one who had lived through a severe economic depression,
Rosalyn soon learned to work for what she needed or wanted; when she
needed braces for her teeth, she earned money by helping her mother sew
neckware. Simon encouraged her in the belief that being a girl did not bar
her from many pursuits that some considered beyond female reach.

Rosalyn, according to her mother, was a determined child with a mind
of her own. She was also precocious. After attending public school number 51
and then 10, both in which she excelled, she enrolled at Walton High School,
where Trudy Elion had studied. After graduation from the latter at 15, Rosalyn, again like Trudy, won admission to Hunter College. Disregarding her
parents' suggestion of a teaching career, Rosalyn decided to become a scientist. "I was a terrible athlete," she recalled, "I couldn't sing, draw, or play the
piano. Science is what I did well." Nuclear physics was coming to the fore at
the time, and she had the good fortune to hear Fermi (see Chapter 15) describe

Rosalyn Yalow
(Courtesy National Library of Medicine
with permission of Rosalyn Yalow.)

nuclear fission when he spoke at Columbia. She graduated from Hunter in 1941 with high honors in chemistry and physics.

Sussman, inspired by the biography of Marie Curie (she admired Henri Becquerel, Pierre Curie, Irene and Frederic Joliot-Curie, too), was determined to become a physicist and also to have a husband and children. Some of her female professors considered her too aggressive and her goals unrealistic. She referred to them as old maids and resolved not to be like them. There were few graduate assistantships available in those days — especially for Jewish women. However, the advent of World War II was beginning to create a shortage of male graduate students, and Sussman eventually obtained an assistantship at the University of Illinois at Urbana-Champaign.

At graduate school the brown-eyed brunette met her future husband. The son of a Syracuse rabbi, Aaron Yalow was studying nuclear physics. They were married on June 6, 1943. The union proved to be a happy one. Rosalyn kept a kosher home and was noted for her cooking. Aaron, who ultimately became a professor of physics, approved of his wife's career. In 1945, she obtained her Ph.D. with a thesis entitled "Doubly Ionized K-Shell Following Radioactive Decay."

The couple decided to live in New York City, where there would be some possibility of work for both of them. Rosalyn's first position was a short stint as an electrical engineer at the Federal Telecommunications Laboratory, where research for the International Telephone and Telegraph was conducted. Within a year, Aaron had found a position in medical physics at Montefiore Hospital. After Rosalyn's job was phased out, she returned to her alma mater, Hunter College, to teach veterans.

During the summer of 1947, when she had no teaching duties, Rosalyn conferred with Edith Quimby, a medical physicist whom she had met through Aaron. The upshot was that Rosalyn was appointed part-time consultant to the Bronx Veterans Administration Hospital, where money was available to set up a radioactivity service. Since she was working in a new field, much improvisation was necessary. According to Rosalyn, "My experience as an electrical engineer was quite useful, in as much as commercial equipment was not readily available: thus much of our early equipment was made by me or according to my design."

By 1946, the nuclear reactor at Oak Ridge, Tennessee, was producing inexpensive isotopes in large quantities. Many believed that isotopes would serve primarily as a cheap replacements for radium in cancer therapy. Yalow had other ideas after reading Georg von Heversy's 1948 book about the use of radioisotopes to study metabolic processes. (It was possible to "tag" a substance with an isotope, administer the tagged substance to an animal or human, then remove the product to a test tube. With appropriate counting instruments and with the proper chemical manipulations, minute quantities of metabolites could be detected by means of their emanation.) She saw great potential in the use of radioisotopes to study biological reactions.

In 1950, Yalow became full-time physicist and chief of the radioisotope service at the V.A. Hospital in the Bronx. Here she met Solomon (known as Sol) Berson, with whom she would collaborate for 22 years. Berson was trained in medicine, a field that had always attracted Yalow. However, she had not tried to enter medical school because she lacked money; she also believed that as a Jewish woman, her chances of admission were slight. Berson's knowledge of biological science complemented her expertise in physics, mathematics and engineering; eventually each taught the other. They worked extremely hard; each commanded respect of the other; each considered the other an equal.

Yalow was happy in her professional life. Regarding her successful career, she once noted: "I wasn't handed college or graduate school or anything else on a silver platter. I had to work very hard, but I did it because I wanted to. That's the real key to happiness." And when asked about her hobbies she replied: "What am I going to do? Ride a bike? Play tennis? This [referring to the laboratory] is where the excitement is."

The pair at first studied the thyroid gland, using radioactive iodine to elucidate the gland's physiology and to diagnose disease. Then they turned their attention to the measurement of such entities as the volume of blood in an individual.

Before the introduction of oral medication to lower the blood sugar, it was thought that almost all diabetics required insulin. Yet it was known that most patients who had developed diabetes in adulthood (type 2 diabetes) produced adequate amounts of insulin. It had been postulated that in such cases, enzymic action destroyed the required insulin. Berson and Yalow decided to test this hypothesis by using iodine-labeled insulin.

In 1956, they gave the labeled insulin to groups of diabetic and nondiabetic subjects, among whom of the latter were schizophrenics treated by insulin shock therapy. It was found that the labeled insulin disappeared more rapidly from the blood plasma of nondiabetics than from that of diabetics.

Further investigation showed that the differences between the two groups was not the disease per se, but rather a previous history of insulin therapy; virtually all insulin-treated subjects developed antibodies to beef-pork insulin. Thus immunity rather than enzymic action was the cause. Until then, it had been believed that the insulin molecule of a different species, because of its low molecular weight, did not produce antibody in the human. Initially publication of the work was opposed, but its importance was soon recognized.

Yalow and her coworker next turned their attention to the insulin antibody. In her own words:

> We then demonstrated that the methods used to determine the concentration of circulating antibody could be used reciprocally to assay the circulating insulin. Thus, radio immunoassay was born.
> Samples of plasma or other body fluids are assayed in a test tube. RIA determines the concentration of an unknown, unlabeled antigen by comparing its inhibitory effect on the binding of radioactively labeled antigen to specific antibody with the inhibitory effect of known standards. The method combines the unparalleled sensitivity with the specificity characteristic of immunological reactions.

RIA could be used to assay hormones, enzymes, viruses, vitamins, drugs and other chemicals; with it there was potential for improved diagnosis and treatment. According to Yalow, useful as the technique was, it was five years before papers written by authors other than she and Berson appeared in the world's literature. The scientific world slowly came to appreciate the value of the new method. RIA eventually led to the creation of less complex analytical methods that use nonradioactive markers.

What of Rosalyn's personal life? A son, Benjamin, was born in 1952 and a daughter, Elanna, two years later. When there were children at home, the family lived very close to the V.A. Hospital. (We recall that Chien-Shiung Wu noted in Chapter 19 that it was important for a mother/scientist to have workplace and home in close proximity.) Rosalyn's philosophy was, "A child must learn from the cradle that upward mobility depends on what people themselves do." Benjamin in time obtained a doctorate in computer science and Elanna one in psychology. Their mother at first wanted them to study medicine, but they had other ideas.

After 18 years with the V.A., Berson moved to Mt. Sinai School of Medicine in New York City to direct internal medicine. He tried to continue his research with Yalow by working nights. He died suddenly in 1972.

As chief of what she named the Solomon A. Berson Research Laboratory, Yalow collaborated with Eugene Strauss, whom she termed "another very talented physician." Together they did high-class research.

As the years passed, the use of RIA in medicine became so common that its international importance could not be overlooked. One half of the 1977

Nobel Prize for physiology or medicine was awarded to Rosalyn Yalow "for the development of radio immunoassay of peptide hormones." The citation stated that the RIA test "was accompanied by a spectacular combination of immunology, isotope research, mathematics, and physics [which has] brought about a revolution in biological and medical research." No doubt Berson would have been a recipient had he lived; some believe that Yalow should have shared her prize money with the Berson family. The other half was divided between Roger Guillemin of the Salk Institute, La Jolla, California, and Andrew Schally of Tulane University and the V.A. Hospital in New Orleans. These two had used RIA in the study of peptide hormone production in humans.

The Yalows flew to Sweden with Elanna and her husband, the latter two having married just two days previously. (Eventually Elanna gave her parents two grandchildren.) Also invited to Stockholm were three students — one from Rosalyn's junior high, one from Walton High School and one from Hunter College. Although she had not always agreed with feminist thinking, when she accepted the Nobel Prize, Rosalyn said:

> ...if women are to start moving toward [equality of opportunity], we must believe in ourselves or no one else will believe in us, we must match our aspirations with competence, courage and determination to succeed, and we must feel a personal responsibility to ease the path for those who come after us. The world cannot afford the loss of the talents of half of its people if we are to solve the many problems that beset us.

She continued to use her status as a Nobel Laureate to express her views. In 1981, she wrote of

> an increasing disillusion leading to the identification of science and scientists with fears of many things including pollution, radiation-induced cancer and destruction of the environment rather than with the real successes of science such as an increase in human lifespan of 25 years since the turn of the century, improved nutrition, and the comforts of modern living. There is at present in the United States a powerful activist movement that is anti-intellectual, anti-science, and antitechnology. If we are to have faith that mankind will survive and thrive on the face of the earth, we must depend on the continued revolutions brought about by science. These are the revolutions that set us free from hunger and disease and permit us to set our sights on the stars. For the future of civilization, we must counter the anti-intellectuals and communicate the glory and excitement of science and discovery to the young.

She was reiterating most of this ten years later. Convinced that scientists should be mothers, she suggested, "Greater effort must be made by society to assume quality care for the children of mothers having aspirations other than remaining in the home while their children are in their developmental years."

Yalow had been awarded the Albert Lasker Medical Research Award in 1975 and was elected to the National Academy of Sciences the following year. It is since she was awarded the Nobel Prize that many other honors have accrued: For example, she has close to 50 honorary doctorates, and the National Medal of Science was presented in 1988. She has also held some professorships and been in demand as a lecturer.

Rosalyn Sussman Yalow claimed, "You can have it all." She explained at an interview how she had it all: "I can't think of anything in the world that I want that I haven't had. I have my marriage, two wonderful children. I have a laboratory that is an absolute joy. I have energy, I have health. As long as there is anything to be done I am never tired."

This energetic woman was coming to work at the V.A. twice a week in 1998. A series of strokes necessitated her official retirement, but she was keeping in touch with what was going on in her field. When asked what, if anything, she would have done differently with her life, her answer was an emphatic "Nothing!"

# Chapter 23

# Mary Good

## *Versatile Chemist*

*Variety's the very spice of life*
*That gives it all its flavor.*
— William Cowper

In 1998, *Chemical and Engineering News* named the "Top 75" individuals — living and dead — from all nations, who have made distinguished contributions to the chemical enterprise during the 75 years of *C&EN's* existence. Among the honorees was Mary Lowe Good, whose accomplishments were described as follows:

> Served in research and leadership positions at Louisiana State University and at Allied Signal; provided science and technology advice and leadership as undersecretary for Technology at the Department of Commerce, member of the National Science Board and Chairman of the President's Council of Advisers on Science and Technology; in ACS (American Chemical Society) as a board member, and as 1987 ACS president.

She was born on June 23, 1931, in Grapevine, Texas, to John W. and Winnie (Mercer) Lowe. Her father was a school superintendent and her mother a teacher. The oldest of four children, Mary grew up in Arkansas. Her high school was so small that neither physics nor chemistry was taught. Mary developed a strong interest in photography and had a dark room in the cellar. When she attended Arkansas State Teachers College (now the University of Central Arkansas in Conway), her intention was to study home economics because at the time, teachers of the subject got extra compensation. However, a beginning chemistry course changed that. "My teacher was an elderly professor who was absolutely fantastic," Mary recalled. By the second semester, she had chosen to major in chemistry. She graduated in 1950, completing the course in three years by enrolling in summer as well as winter classes.

She immediately began graduate study at the University of Arkansas in Fayetteville. In 1950, she married Billy Jewel Good, a graduate student in physics. (Forty-five years later, she referred to him as an understanding and helpful husband.) She received her master's degree in chemistry in 1953 and her doctorate two years later. Fellowship money saw her through.

Mary's first postdoctoral position was at Louisiana State University in Baton Rouge. She entered academe for two reasons: first, Bill Jewel wanted to earn his Ph.D. in physics, a program offered at LSU; second, the hours were more flexible than in an industrial situation. The latter was important to Mary because she then had a son, Billy John, who was nine months old. James Patrick was born five years later. Their mother recalled that she had good in-house (not live-in) domestic help. She remained a faculty member in the LSU system until 1980. In 1974, she had obtained the rank of Boyd Professor of Chemistry at the New Orleans campus and Boyd Professor of Materials Science in the division of engineering research at the Baton Rouge campus in 1978. During her tenure at LSU, she wrote 92 papers and a book. According to her, she enjoyed working with the students, and she still keeps in touch with many of the graduate students who worked with her.

While at LSU, Mary also became very active in working in positions of responsibility for the American Chemical Society. To illustrate, as chairman of the Board of Directors, she had charge of an $159 million budget. Her services to the Society culminated in her election to the presidency in 1987.

After 15 years in a university setting, Good entered industry, accepting the position as vice president and director of research at UOP Inc. in Des Plaines, Illinois, then one of the Signal companies that handled chemicals. Her career was influenced by various mergers that the company made. She attributed her success to a willingness to take on existing challenges and to use the people already working with her to help her to succeed. By 1986, she was senior vice president for technology and located in Morristown, New Jersey, where Allied Signal had a facility. Good's area of responsibility involved 500 people and some $75 million earmarked for research and technology. She referred to her position as a very high-pressure, high-profile job.

About this time, she noted:

> Both biotechnology and materials science depend on our ability to manipulate chemical structure. Chemical structure determines the components of all inanimate objects, shapes all forms of life, masterminds our thoughts and actions, dictates health or illness, orders happiness or despair, enriches or impoverishes nations.
>
> We can better understand this condition if we face it in a global context. A world economy has developed in which every country must compete in global markets to sustain internal growth and economic stability.

In keeping with this, during her years in industry, Good had held science advisory posts in the administrations of Jimmy Carter, Ronald Reagan and George Bush. Then in 1993, she accepted a full-time position as undersecretary for technology in the Clinton Administration. Her department is responsible for making clear to the public the scope and importance of the federal investment in scientific research and development. Good made these remarks in 1996:

> The public believes that science and technology is a top government priority. That means, at the very least, maintaining the current level of funding for research and development. Without our share of research, development and high technology manufacturing, it would be very difficult to provide the high-quality jobs and wealth creation required to assume a responsible standard of living for our children and grandchildren.

**Mary Good**

**(Reprinted with permission from *C& EN News*, May 1996, Vol. 74, #20, 1996 American Chemical Society)**

She has been affiliated with and active in many professional societies such as the International Union of Pure and Applied Chemistry. She has also received numerous honorary degrees and honors, including the Priestley Medal (1997) from the American Chemical Society for distinguished services to chemistry.

Fly-fishing is one of Mary's hobbies. Along with Scottish history, she lists, not surprisingly, national and international technology and economic policy as interests.

Since 1965, she has been a member of Zonta International, a service organization for business and professional women. Zonta awards graduate scholarships in aerospace science in memory of Amelia Earhart, a former Zontian. From 1971 to 1988, Good served as chairman of the Earhart Awards Committee. Her experience should hearten those who despair of women entering science: at first, few candidates had the necessary credentials. Then in the mid–1980s, there were more than 300 exceptionally well-qualified candidates from many nations. She considers that a real mirror of how opportunities for women in education and science have changed.

What of Good's plans for retirement? She plans to "help start a venture capital firm for early-stage technology-intensive companies in Arkansas; serve on a few corporate boards; and continue to speak for and work with groups interested in U.S. technology policy."

What, if anything, would she have done differently? "Probably nothing," is her answer. "I have had a wonderful life, both personally and profession-ally."

Mary Lowe Good's varied and successful professional career exemplifies opportunities open to women as the twenty-first century approaches. On the personal side, her marriage has lasted; she takes pride in her two sons — the older directs wetlands programs in Louisiana, the younger works with inter-national refugees. She considers her four grandchildren her legacy.

Here are her comments for women scientists:

• Working in a science or technology career is highly rewarding. Almost always the work is exciting and fun even when it is most challenging.

• Careers develop best when not tightly planned. If one is flexible, takes the best opportunity open at the time, works hard and has the courage to move when a better opportunity arises, one's career will progress.

• Having children early in a career when one's work is not so visible or demanding is a plus. Also they get to grow up with you and they have a much more realistic view of what will be required for their own success.

• Picking a husband is probably the most important career choice one will ever make!

# Epilogue

A comparison of the subjects of this book might give some clue(s) to attaining success as a scientist.

The immediate families of these women were unusually supportive, and sometimes an uncle or grandfather provided crucial help. The exception is perhaps the Hyman family; fortunately for Libbie, a high school teacher who knew her academic capabilities found financial assistance. Little information is known about Nettie Stevens' background, but there appeared to be no family opposition to her goals. Many of the families were advanced in their thinking about women's education, particularly those of Chien-Shiung Wu and Maria Goeppert Mayer. Although Barbara McClintock's mother and the fathers of Karen Horney and Rita Levi-Montalcini favored marriage over career, they supported their daughters' decisions. Generally speaking, educated and enlightened parents instilled in their offspring a love of learning. Six of the twenty-three women had Jewish backgrounds; the Jewish respect for knowledge must have had an effect on these scientists. The majority of the families lived or had lived in comfortable circumstances. However, as demonstrated by Rosalyn Yalow and Gertrude Elion, lack of money was not, in the long run, a deterrent.

Of interest is the strong attachment to music on the part of some of the women. (It probably only demonstrates that the Biblical proverb — "Train up a child in the way he should go, and when he is old, he will not depart" — sometimes is correct.) We recall that McClintock studied harmony and played the banjo in a college band; Annie Cannon and Florence Sabin were accomplished musicians; the Apgar family gave concerts on the spur of the moment. Most of the women had a deep appreciation of music, an appreciation that culminated in Gertrude Elion's passion for opera. At the other extreme, music was not important in the life of Florence Bascom — possibly because her father did not regard it as so.

There is much evidence that these women possessed superior mental capacity. Annie Jump Cannon's performance in high school led her teachers to suggest to Mr. Cannon that his daughter would benefit from a college education. Libbie Hyman was the valedictorian as well as the youngest member of her high school class. Mary Swartz Rose also was the valedictorian of her high school class. Rosalyn Yalow graduated from high school at 15. Chien-Shiung Wu finished high school with high honors. Gerty Cori and Karen Horney were products of the highly-rated gymnasium system. Mayer passed the demanding abitur with no difficulty. Both Yalow and Elion gained entrance to Hunter College by taking very stiff competitive examinations.

Possessing an advanced degree is commonly considered an indication of academic ability or of tremendous persistence on the part of one with an average IQ. Fifteen of the subjects held Ph.D.s or honorary doctorates, eight had MDs, Helen Taussig earning that degree despite dyslexia. Virginia Apgar was elected to Alpha Omega Alpha, which is a medical school's equivalent of a college's Phi Beta Kappa.

Religion played an outstanding role in nineteenth century life. In the cases at hand, it had a relatively minor role, as might be expected in the twentieth century. Religion, however, was important to Cornelia Clapp, Alice Hamilton and Virginia Apgar. Karen Horney struggled to find a true religion. Barbara McClintock studied Tibetan Buddhism.

Related to religion, there was often a desire to bring about social reform, as was seen in Alice Hamilton. Other active reformers, but apparently less religious, were Josephine Baker, Florence Sabin and Rachel Carson. These three physicians were instrumental in bringing about reform that was related to their profession of medicine, Carson to hers as a biologist.

Noted for their pacifist views were Clapp and Hamilton.

The right to vote was an important issue for women in the early decades of the twentieth century. While Sabin and Baker worked for women's suffrage, the others did not give it such active support. It is probable that their work left them with little time to do much else.

To include marriage and children in a successful career is a continuing problem for women. Nine of the women married: Horney, Rose, Cori, Mayer, Hopper, Wu, Sager, Yalow and Good. Horney's marriage ended in divorce, as did Hopper's. The remaining seven had devoted spouses, all scientists themselves who understood their wives' work. The Coris brought to mind the Curies — each a husband-and-wife team that won a Nobel Prize. The marriages produced children except in the cases of Hopper and Sager. As the twentieth century progressed, women were beginning to think like Yalow — that they could have it all.

There was potential for gender discrimination when a husband and wife team worked at the same institution. For example, when Mayer began her career at the University of Chicago as a volunteer professor, her husband received a salary for his services. She put up with the situation because it enabled her to work in an academic setting in the company of scientists whom she respected.

Even when there is no gender discrimination, marriage may impose career restraints that a couple must work out. For instance, when a young Mary Good looked for a position, she sought and found a location where her husband could work on a Ph.D. in physics.

Although these women did not belong to "old boy" networks, in some cases they received much support from their male colleagues. Mayer and McClintock in particular benefited from this.

Libbie Hyman felt discriminated against in the botany department at the University of Chicago, not because she was a woman, but because she was a Jew.

In 1997, *C&EN* stated that Good was the first woman to receive the Priestley Medal. Some women believe that such information should be pointed out; others think it better to assume that men and women are judged together and that the best person, regardless of gender, is chosen. As more and more women enter science, surely it will not be news that a woman is highly honored for professional achievements; women should have confidence in Apgar's contention that when you're good, you're good.

For people in academic positions, teaching is part of the job — at the least, graduate students have to be supervised, resident doctors have to be trained, and so on. Some institutions require professors to participate in undergraduate instruction. This is usually unpopular because it interferes with research activities. It is important of course that coming generations be taught well. Generally speaking, the women seem to have done very well in teaching. Clapp, Stevens, Bascom, Sabin, Rose, Wu, Hopper and Elion taught as a stepping stone to specific careers. Much credit is due Clapp and Stevens for instituting good departments in top women's colleges. Also, Rose set up a new department of nutrition in a respected university. Sabin proved to be an outstanding teacher of medical students, encouraging them to experiment. In contrast, teaching undergraduates was not McClintock's forte or interest.

It cannot truly be known if the women's chosen careers benefitted their health. However, it is remarkable that of the 17 who died before this writing, seven lived more than 80 years; one died at 90 and one at 101.

Each one of the subjects showed an enthusiasm for her work. As examples, Cannon was still working when she died at 77; at 88, Hamilton declared she wouldn't have changed her life a bit; the interest that Sabin brought to her research carried over to her public career; Barbara McClintock was still doing research at 90; and when she was over 60, Apgar returned to Hopkins to learn about modern genetics.

They also showed perseverance, with McClintock and Sager as prime examples — each had to wait years until her ideas were accepted. Levi-Montalcini, also, did not receive the credit she deserved for many years. Probably the perseverance was related to enthusiasm; surely the efforts of Cannon and Hyman, for example, would have flagged had the women not had real interest in their projects. Yalow admitted to working very hard during her professional life "because I wanted to." To a greater or lesser extent this was true of all of them.

Chance, of course, played a role. The long Depression of the 1930s lessened the likelihood of employment, no matter the qualifications. World War II and the Cold War that followed led to the development of nuclear physics, and with it, opportunities not available until then. For example, Mayer, who was exceptionally well qualified in quantum mechanics, was not employed by Johns Hopkins during the Depression. Her husband, however, was a member of the faculty. Later she was hired to work at the Argonne National Laboratory where atomic research was being conducted and where her expertise was needed. (Argonne is operated by the U.S. Atomic Energy Commission and the University of Chicago.) Situations like this are fortuitous and could happen again.

By 1985, the U.S. Navy had bestowed the rank of rear admiral on mathematician Grace Hopper. This should convince the cynics that the last roadblocks to female advancement are disappearing. Mary Good's career underscores the fact that at the end of the twentieth century, there are few bars to women scientists.

Thus it can be presumed that in the twenty-first century, a woman with adequate mental capacity, a penchant for hard work and the resolve to endure can have a satisfying career — intellectually and financially — if she is willing to let that career fill a major role in her life. Words from twentieth century women scientists may guide her:

> *The selection of work in which one delights and a diligent adherence to it, are main ingredients of success.* — Florence Bascom

> *Picking a husband is probably the most important career choice one will ever make.* — Mary Good

> *You can do anything you have to.* — Libbie Hyman

# Bibliography

Apgar, V., and J. Beck. *Is My Baby All Right?: A Guide to Birth Defects.* New York: Trident Press, 1972.

Arnold, L.B. *Four Lives in Science: Women's Education in the Nineteenth Century.* New York: Schoken Books, 1984.

Baldwin, J. *To Heal the Heart of a Child: Helen Taussig.* New York: Walker, 1992.

Bascom, F. "The University in 1874–1887." *Wisconsin's Magazine of History* 8 (March 1925): 300–08.

Berson, S.A. et al. "Insulin-I$^{131}$ Metabolism in Human Subjects: Demonstration of Insulin-Binding Globulin in the Circulation of Insulin Treated Subjects." *Clinical Investigation* 35 (1956): 170–190.

_____, and R. Yalow. "General Principles of Radioimmunoassay." *Clinica Chimica. Acta* 22 (1968): 51–69.

Biermann, C.A. Entry on Ruth Sager. *Women in the Biological Sciences: A Bibliographic Source Book.* Westport, CT: Greenwood Press, 1997.

Billings, C. *Grace Hopper: Navy Admiral and Computer Pioneer.* Hillside, NJ: Enslow, 1989.

*Biographical Cyclopaedia of American Women.* Detroit: Gale Research, 1974 (reprint of an annual periodical).

Blackwelder, R. "In Memoriam Libbie Henrietta Hyman, 1889–1969." *Journal of Biological Psychology* 32 (1970): 1–15.

Blalock, A., and H. Taussig. "The Surgical Treatment of Malformations of the Heart." *Journal of the American Medical Association.* 128, No. 3 (May 19, 1945) 189–202.

Bluemel, E. *Florence Sabin: Colorado Woman of the Century.* Boulder: University of Colorado Press, 1959.

Brush, S. "Nettie M. Stevens and the Discovery of Sex Determination by Chromosomes." *Isis* 59, No. 274 (June, 1978): 162–70.

Cannon, A.J. "Sarah Frances Whiting." *Popular Astronomy* XXXV, No. 10, (December 1927): 538–45.

Carr, E.P. "One Hundred Years of Science at Mount Holyoke College." *Mount Holyoke College Alumnae Quarterly* XX, No. 3 (November 1936): 135–38.

Carson, R. *The Sea Around Us.* New York: Oxford University Press, 1951.

_____. *Silent Spring.* Boston: Houghton Mifflin, 1962.

Cohen, S., and J.A. Shapiro. "Transposable Genetic Elements." *Scientific American* 242, No. 2 (February 1980): 40–9.

"Contributions to the Chemical Enterprise: C&EN's Top 75." *Chemical & Engineering News.* (January 12, 1998): 171–85.

Creighton, H.B. and B. McClintock. "A Correlation of Cytological and Genetical Crossing-over in *Zea Mays.*" *Proceedings of the National Academy of Sciences* 17, No. 1 (1931): 492–97.

*Current Biography.* "Mayer, Maria Goeppert" (1964): 287–89; "Levi-Montalcini, Rita" (1989): 344–48; "Wu, Chien-Shiung" (1959): 491–92; "Yalow, Rosalyn S[ussman]" (1978): 458–60.

Darnell, J., et al. *Molecular Cell Biology*. New York: Scientific American Books, 1990.

Dash, J. *A Life of One's Own: Three Gifted Women and the Men They Married.* New York: Harper & Row, 1973.

_____. *The Triumph of Discovery: Women Scientists Who Won the Nobel Prize.* New York: Messner, 1991.

Diefendorf, E., ed. *The New York Public Library's Books of the Century.* New York: Oxford University Press, 1996.

Eagles, J.A., et al. *Mary Swartz Rose 1874–1941: Pioneer in Nutrition.* New York: Teachers College Press, 1979.

Felder, D.C. *100 Most Influential Women of All Time.* New York: Carol Publishing Group, 1996.

Gleasner, D.C. *Breakthrough: Women in Science.* New York: Walker, 1984.

Good, M.L., ed. *Biotechnology and Materials Science.* Washington, D.C.: American Chemical Society, 1988.

Grant, M.P. *Alice Hamilton: Pioneer Doctor in Industrial Medicine.* New York: Abelard-Schuman, 1967.

Grun, B. *The Timetables of History.* New York: Simon and Schuster, 1979.

Hamilton, A. "Angels of Victory." *The New Republic.* (June 25, 1919): 244–45.

_____. *Exploring the Dangerous Trades: The Autobiography of Alice Hamilton.* Boston: Northeastern University Press, 1985 (originally published 1943).

Haywood, C. "A Scientific Heritage." *Mount Holyoke Alumnae Quarterly* XLIII, No. 3 (Fall 1925): 122–25.

Hitchings, G.B., and G.B. Elion. "Layer on Layer: The Bruce F. Cain Memorial Award Lecture." *Cancer Research* 45 (June 1985): 2415–20.

Holloway, M. "Profile: Gertrude Belle Elion." *Scientific American* (October 1991): 40+.

Hyman, P.E., and D. D. Moore, eds. *Jewish Women in America: An Historical Encyclopedia.* New York: Routledge, 1997.

James, E.T., et al. eds. *Notable American Women 1607–1950: A Biographical Dictionary.* Cambridge, MA: Belknap Press 1971.

Kass-Simon, G., and P. Farnes, eds. *Women of Science: Righting the Record.* Bloomington: Indiana University Press, 1993.

Keller, E.F. *A Feeling for the Organism: The Life and Work of Barbara McClintock.* San Francisco: W.H. Freeman, 1983.

_____. *Reflections on Gender and Science.* New Haven, CT: Yale University Press, 1985.

Kihss, P. Article on Josephine Baker. *New York World-Telegram* (January 21, 1942): 21.

Lear, L. *Rachel Carson: Witness for Nature.* New York: Henry Holt, 1997.

Levi-Montalcini, R. (tr. by Luigi Atturdi) *In Praise of Imperfection: My Life and Work.* New York: Basic Books, 1988.

_____, and P. Calissano. "The Nerve-Growth Factor." *Scientific American* (1979): 68–77.

Long, J.R. "Priestley Medal." *Chemical & Engineering News* (May 13 1996): 36–38.

McGrayne, S.B. *Nobel Prize Women in Science: Their Lives, Struggles, and Momentous Discoveries.* New York: Carol Publishing Group, 1993.

McHenry, R., ed. *Famous American Women: A Biographical Dictionary from Colonial Times to the Present.* New York: Dover 1983 (originally published in 1980 as *Liberty's Women*).

McMaster, P.D., and M. Heidelberger. "Florence Rena Sabin." *Biographical Memoirs.* National Academy of Sciences. New York: Columbia University Press XXXIV (1960): 271–305.

"Mary Good." *The Scientist.*Vol. 10, No. 19 (September 1996): 30.

Mayer, M.G. "The Structure of the Nucleus." *Scientific American.* (March 1951): 22–26.

_____. Autobiography for Les Prix Nobel. Niels Bohr Library. American Institute of Physics, 1962.

Morgan, A.L., et al. "Cornelia Maria Clapp." *Mount Holyoke Alumnae Quarterly* XIX, No. 1 (May 1935): 1–9.

Morgan, T.H. "The Scientific Work of Miss N.M. Stevens." *Science* XXXVI, No. 928 (October 11, 1912) 468–470.

Nilsson, M. "Nobel Committee Refutes Allegations of Corruption." *Lancet* Vol. 346 (September 16, 1995): 763–64.

Ogilvie, I.H. "Obituary — Florence Bascom." *Science* 102, No. 2648 (September 28, 1945): 320–21.

_____, and Gray, H.L. "In Memoriam: Florence Bascom." *Bryn Mawr Alumnae Bulletin* (November 1945): 12–13.

Ogilvie, M.B., and C.L. Choquette. "Nettie Maria Stevens: Her Life and Contributions to Cytogenetics." *Proceedings of the American Philosophical Society* 125, No. 4 (August 1981): 292–311.

Opfell, O.S. *The Lady Laureates: Women Who Have Won the Nobel Prizes,* 2d ed. Metuchen, NJ : Scarecrow, 1986.

Paris, B.J. *Karen Horney: A Psychologist's Search for Self-Understanding.* New Haven, CT: Yale University Press, 1994.

Phelan, M.K. *Probing the Unknown: The Story of Dr. Florence Sabin.* New York: Dell, 1969.

Quinn, S. *A Mind of Her Own: The Life of Karen Horney.* New York: Summit Books, 1987.

Ranahan, D.C. *Contributions of Women: Medicine.* Minneapolis: Dillon Press, 1981.

Rayner-Asham, M.F., and G.W. Rayner-Asham. *A Devotion to Their Science: Pioneer Women of Radioactivity.* Philadelphia: Chemical Heritage Foundation, 1997.

Reynolds, M. D. *Women Champions of Human Rights: Eleven U.S. Leaders of the Twentieth Century.* Jefferson, NC: McFarland, 1991.

Rossiter, M.W. *Women Scientists in America: Struggles and Strategies to 1940.* Baltimore: The Johns Hopkins University Press, 1982.

_____. *Women Scientists in America: Before Affirmative Action 1940–1972.* Baltimore: The Johns Hopkins University Press, 1995.

Rubin, J.L. *Karen Horney: Gentle Rebel of Psychoanalysis.* New York: Dial Press, 1978.

Sachs, R.B. "Maria Goeppert Mayer." *Biographical Memoirs.* (National Academy of Sciences) 50 (1979): 311–28.

Sager. R. "Genes Outside the Chromosomes." *Scientific American* 212 (January 1965): 71–79.

_____. *Cytoplasmic Genes and Organelles.* New York: Academic Press, 1972.

_____, and F.J. Ryan. *Cell Heredity.* New York: John Wiley and Sons, 1961.

Shapley, H. "Address in Memory of Annie Jump Cannon." *The Wellesley Magazine* (June 1941): 446–47.

Shearer, B.F., and B.S. Shearer, eds. *Notable Women in the Life Sciences: A Biographical Dictionary.* Westport, CT: Greenwood, 1996.

Sicherman, B., and C.H. Green, eds. *Notable American Women: The Modern Period.* Cambridge, MA: Belknap Press, 1980.

_____. *Alice Hamilton: A Life in Letters.* Cambridge, MA: Harvard University Press, 1984.

Smith, E.F. *The Stone Lady: A Memoir of Florence Bascom.* Bryn Mawr, PA: Bryn Mawr College, 1981.

Stone, E. "A Mme. Curie from the Bronx." *The New York Times Magazine* (April 8, 1978): 29+.

Sturtevant, A.S, *A History of Genetics.* New York: Harper & Row, 1965.

*The Telescope* VIII, No. 3 (May-June 1941); issue in memory of Annie Jump Cannon.

Turk, D.C., and I.A. Porter. *A Short Textbook of Medical Microbiology.* Chicago: Year Book Medical Publishers, 1973.

Vivian, T. *Pioneering Research in Surgical Shock and Cardiovascular Surgery: An Autobiography.* Philadelphia: University of Pennsylvania Press, 1985.

Westkott, M. *The Feminist Legacy of Karen Horney.* New Haven, CT: Yale University Press, 1986.

Yalow, R.S. "Radioactivity in the Service of Man." *BioScience* 31 (January 1981): 23–8.

_____, and S.A. Berson. "Assay of Plasma Insulin in Human Subjects by Immunological Methods." *Nature* (Nov. 21, 1959): 1648–49.

_____, and S.A. Berson. "Immunoassay of Endogenous Plasma Insulin in Man." *Journal of Clinical Investigation* 39 (1960): 1157–75.

Yost, E. *American Women of Science.* Philadelphia: Frederick A. Stokes, 1943.

_____. *Women of Modern Science.* New York: Dodd, Mead, 1952.


Personal communications with:

Gertrude Elion
Abbot Gaunt
Mary Good
John McClaughry
Arthur Pardee
Rosalyn Yalow

# Index

Numbers in boldface type indicate photographs.